STORIES FROM THE DEEP

Reflections on a Life Exploring Ireland's North Atlantic Waters

KEN O'SULLIVAN

Gill Books
Hume Avenue
Park West
Dublin 12
www.gillbooks.ie
Gill Books is an imprint of M.H. Gill and Co.

© Ken O'Sullivan 2019
978 07171 865 2 5

Designed by Studio 10 Design
Edited by Djinn von Noorden
Proofread by Neil Burkey
Printed by Gutenberg Press, Malta
This book is typeset in Goudy
All photos © Ken O'Sullivan unless otherwise stated

The map on page 219 was developed by the Marine
Institute and Geological Survey Ireland under the
INFOMAR programme which is mapping the physical,
chemical and biological features of Ireland's seabed
and is funded by the Department of Communications,
Climate Action and Environment (DCCAE).

*The paper used in this book comes from the wood pulp of
managed forests. For every tree felled, at least one tree is
planted, thereby renewing natural resources.*

All rights reserved.
No part of this publication may be copied, reproduced
or transmitted in any form or by any means, without
written permission of the publishers.

A CIP catalogue record for this book is available from
the British Library.

5 4 3 2 1

To my mother Rita Garvey, and my sisters
Catherine, Margaret, Marie and Eleanor,
strong women who sustained us all.

To our dear brother Liam, too beautiful
for this world.

For
Katrina, Eimear, Jill & Aishling,
lights that will keep shining.

~~~~~~

Thanks to:
Mike Hilliard Mulcahy
Jim Cooney
Tom Mulcahy
John Richardson
Conor Nagle at Gill Publishing
Mícheál Ó Cinnéide
Gay Cooke RIP my English teacher
And all the pain we suffered which led us
reflect and create, and without which we
might have been more balanced,
contented people.

CONTENTS

THE SEA AND ME

MY MOTHER TOLD ME I was born dehydrated. Her waters had broken well before my delivery, 'You looked so dried out, almost dishevelled,' she told me fondly. I've always loved water. One of my earliest recollections is being bathed in the porcelain kitchen sink in our old house in Ennis, laughing as my mother poured jugs of warm water over my head and me splashing and loving the droplets of water slipping through my tiny hands.

I grew up swimming in the Turret, a pool in the River Fergus on the outskirts of town. There were diving boards there, but the council took them down, probably after being sued by someone. So we climbed the trees on the riverbank and jumped in from there. I remember midnight summer swims, six or seven of us skinny-dipping in the dark and just laughing at the sheer joy of it.

In my last January there, I cycled to and from school across a bridge overlooking the Turret. I watched the swollen winter river gurgle up like a dark, devilish volcano, troubled waters … it seemed to reflect my failing exam results and the worry and pressure I was under, a few months before the torturous life-defining exam every Irish teenager has to face.

Summer was golden. Warm evenings in the Turret when everyone was in good form, I watched a fella a year older than me, who'd just finished school, swim across the river, lay back and rest on shallow sunken rocks under the trees. God, I wished that was me, another year of that shite. I hated school from day one, and it never leaves you, I still have nightmares about that exam, it's the night before the Leaving Cert Irish and I've nothing done, it's terrifying, I wake up in a sweat. But my time eventually came around and I swam triumphantly across the river to rest in the warm shallow water of a golden July evening.

Then there was the sea. My father would pack what seemed like six or seven of us into a car and we'd drive the twenty-one miles to Lahinch. Maybe because we only went a few times a year, these were the really special days. There are a couple of small hills on the road as you approach Lahinch, we'd be bursting with anticipation, and over the years someone came up with a game of who could see the sea first as we rose up the last hill, to steal a distant glance at the blue Atlantic horizon, 'I see the sea,' 'No you don't,' as if the excitement weren't already enough.

At first the sea is freezing, we wail and jump, arms wrapped around ourselves inching into deeper water. Teeth chattering, sinking cautiously into the bracing waves, then more screams. And in no time we've forgotten the cold, jumping over waves and splashing each other for what seems like hours, then we're in the reverse situation of not wanting to embrace the land, just another few minutes, *ple-eee-ase*.

I remember salty faces and hair and sandy toes as we piled back into the car. On the way home we'd stop a couple of miles along the road in Ennistymon for canned sweets – boiled glassy sweets that an old woman would fill into brown paper bags, 'sixpence-worth please', and back in the car we'd doze on the soft, briny tiredness that only the sea brings. The sea stays with you.

~~~~~~~~

My father came from Fenit Island, Co. Kerry, where our family had lived since about 1750. I was fortunate to spend the summers of my youth there in what I can only describe as a Huckleberry Finn-type existence, because on Fenit Island, we had the sea every day.

When I was ten or eleven years old and I had just got the fishing bug, most things in my world were things that got in the way of just being on the rocks at Béal Gheal, Oiléain na Choise or Cloichín or any of the other colourful place names thought up by my ancestors for the fishing spots around the island. Approaching the shore on the back of my uncle's small red tractor, there was only one word I dreaded, swell. As the sea came into view, with a black foreboding sky bearing down on it, I could see the slow, deliberate rise of darkened water engulfing the rocks and the ensuing gurgling of white water. Shaking his head, my uncle said the dreaded word, swell … too much swell today, boy. It's funny how a word can conjure up so much imagery. When my father stood watching the sea and sombrely used that word, I understood about the people who had drowned here on our island.

You see Irish coastal folks had mastered so much of surviving on the seashore; they became expert fishermen, if only on a subsistence scale. Some of the earliest evidence of human presence in Ireland has been found on our shores; I've found 6,000-year-old shell middens on the Clare coast with thousands of limpet shells and a black 'cooking stone'. But getting into the sea was not something these folks did well; they just couldn't.

I spent much of my teenage summers on Fenit Island with my father, fishing, pulling trammel nets out of freezing pre-dawn waters, and picking periwinkles and carrageen, which we'd then sell in Tralee. Hard work, but it brought a great sense of purpose, of harvest and subsistence and self-dependence. In my experience, rural farm folk – but most especially island people – had an incredible ability of self-reliance: they could make almost anything they needed, simply because they had to, and perhaps those who couldn't didn't survive or left. We slept in the airy rooms of my uncles' farmhouse, which smelt of well, farm, and salty air, under covers made of cotton washed ashore in the 1920s from a shipwreck and made into quilts by my grandmother long before we knew what a continental quilt was. They were still in use when my uncle Jack, the last of our kind on Fenit Island, died in 1994.

There was a deep sense of peace and calm to island life, everything slowed down, and time was dictated only by the morning and evening milking of cows and the stages of the tide. My uncle Den would ask me to check the paper to see what time 'high water' was today, if he had to go to town, the mainland could only be accessed across the strand at low tide. My father had, on retirement, returned to the seashore of his

OPPOSITE: *Compass jellyfish off the Clare coast*

own youth, to do the things he had done with his father back in the 1920s and '30s, ancient fishing methods and local knowledge handed down.

He bought a trammel net and 'mounted it', running ropes through the bottom and top rows of mesh. Three-inch tubular lead weights were placed on the bottom rope and squeezed in place with large pliers, floats were placed about every half yard on the top row. We'd tie rocks onto the ropes at either end of the net and at low tide row out into maybe a fathom of water. My father would slowly feed the net out from the back of the boat as I rowed parallel to the shore until we reached the end of the net, which was over a hundred yards long before mounting, but would condense to maybe eighty yards as the lead weights stretched it down into the water. And then we'd wait. And wonder and worry if all would be OK with our net.

Towards high tide with the water now deeper than the net, fish would swim under and around it to feed in the shallows, where they'd remain in the falling tide, by which time they were trapped and their desperate exertions for freedom would only tighten the mesh around them.

The trammel net caught everything: crabs, jellyfish, dabs, plaice, dogfish or 'calaheens' as my father called them. With their sandpaper skin they were tough to get out of a net, and my father would give them a belt on his knee, as if in admonishment, before throwing them back. We even caught that ugliest of fish, the monkfish (angler fish), which we threw back into the sea, and I was amazed and amused to discover years later, living in London, that people not only ate them, but that they were one of the most prized and expensive of fish.

Our trophy catch was the sea trout; the sight of its shiny body flashing in the net, sparkling at us like a gold nugget dug deep from an unwilling ground was the ultimate prize, a feast for our family. But more than anything the trammel net caught seaweed, all kinds of seaweed, and if you didn't clean it all off immediately it soon became like wire, making it impossible to remove.

I remember cleaning a net for hours and getting sick of it; my father must have noticed my self-pity. 'Do you see the tracks on those rocks, son?' he said, lighting his pipe, and he pointed to grooves perhaps three or four inches deep and about a yard and a half apart that ran the along the stone foreshore at Cuan Éamainn storm beach on the south-west side of the island. 'Those tracks were worn down by the wheels of your grandparents' and great-grandparents' pony and trap, hauling seaweed out to the mainland to sell.'

How many trips did it take to wear stone down four inches?

My father always told me it was the sea that helped our people to survive the Famine, when millions of Irish people died or emigrated due to the failure of the potato crop – their staple food at a time of already great huger and suffering. Winter herring, summer bass and mackerel, year-round pollack, cockles and periwinkles all provided nutrition. They'd even stand for hours in shallow sandy water with a pitchfork, gently probing for plaice or other flat fish, a real feast – the sand would suddenly kick and the shallow water tear up as the prong pierced a fish.

Seaweeds such as dillisk and carrageen were natural sources of essential vitamins and so the ability of many island and coastal folks to harvest food from the sea sustained them to a large degree.

My father swam throughout the winter some years and talked of diving down between lobsters and giant pollack, though I'm afraid I doubt he did, for in the days before masks and wetsuits in Ireland no one got to really explore the undersea world, the same world that had provided for them for centuries.

We live in a time of great fortuity then, thanks in no small part to neoprene, the synthetic rubber used in wetsuits and developed by the genius chemist Wallace Carothers in the late 1920s. Carothers was an instructor in organic chemistry at Harvard University and his pioneering work and ability came to the attention of The DuPont Corporation who apparently pursued him until he agreed to leave his Harvard post. Rubber had become a strategically important raw material, particularly because of its military usage, since armies moved on vehicles that rolled on rubber.

Wars were fought over rubber sources in places such as The Congo and Borneo, the notion of the 'Wild Man of Borneo' is deeply ironic, for people in Borneo never experienced anything like the barbaric, senseless destruction wreaked on them by foreign white men and their armies of colonialism. All for power and rubber.

Developing a synthetic form of rubber would be of major strategic and national importance, and so Carothers and his team at DuPont set to work in 1927 and over several years developed the polymers that would become chloroprene and later neoprene, the material used in wetsuits – although it would take decades for them to become the easy-fitting suits we have today. By 1934 Carothers' team had also developed nylon and polyester, quite staggering achievements in a few short years, given how these materials have changed all our lives.

Tragically, Wallace Carothers took his own life aged just 37, feeling he had betrayed the ideals of chemistry and achieved little, but Wallace suffered from severe depression. I do wish he could have known of the joy he brought to so many people, and the change of consciousness his work has facilitated through our ability to now truly experience and document the under-water world.

~~~~~~~

Thanks to Wallace it was with a sense of triumph that I returned after many years to my father's home place and spent long days swimming and diving in all the waters in which I had been warned never to swim.

Entering the underwater world is elation in itself, weightless and drifting, time slows down among the beautiful creatures and habitats. In Ireland we are blessed with temperate seas, perhaps the most fertile on the planet. To experience plains of vibrant red

Moon jellyfish

seaweeds, hypnotically swaying in swell, or shoals of pulsating moon jellyfish, many thousands of them in breeding colours drawing ever closer together, is wonder in itself. In the waters around Fenit Island I meet dogfish, calaheens swimming gracefully through the kelp or resting, gills pulsing, monkfish decoratively camouflaged within the weed, waving their lures to catch small fish, and even inquisitive blue sharks with their Teddy boy-like heads exploring everything; in truth it is difficult to articulate in a way that actually conveys the magic of the place. So different from what I saw dead and dying in fishing nets.

Moments into my first ever scuba dive in Byron Bay, Australia, I am flabbergasted by the beauty, colour and feel of this dreamlike underwater world; you have to dive to experience the three-dimensionality, to truly feel what it's like to be here, looking up at the underside of the sea surface, glassy and mirror-like. It's as if you've crossed over into a hallucinogenic Alice-in-Wonderland world, without the drugs. The French have a beautiful saying, *avoir un coup de foudre*, literally 'to have a bolt of lightning', but they use it in the context of romance to mean love at first sight. My first ocean dive was this, and unconsciously I said to myself, oh how my father would have loved this.

And so, after many years of exploring the ocean and underwater world around Ireland, I became an underwater cameraman and film-maker and spent years trying to learn my craft and master all the skills and challenges an independent film-maker faces, the technology of cameras and water housings, of scuba and freediving and sea conditions, of editing and software and trying to get documentaries funded, of reaching some or other plateau where your competency allows the release of the story within you and its many facets, and at some or other point releasing and revealing your stories to the world. And no one was more surprised than myself that people liked them.

~~~~~~

I'm ten metres down in the blue waters of the mid-Atlantic, my lungs bursting for air as I rise gently for the surface; a leviathan has just swum a couple of metres beneath me, all 90 feet of him taking 27 seconds to pass – a blue whale, the largest animal ever

Diving to a blue whale. PHOTO: STEFANO ULIVI

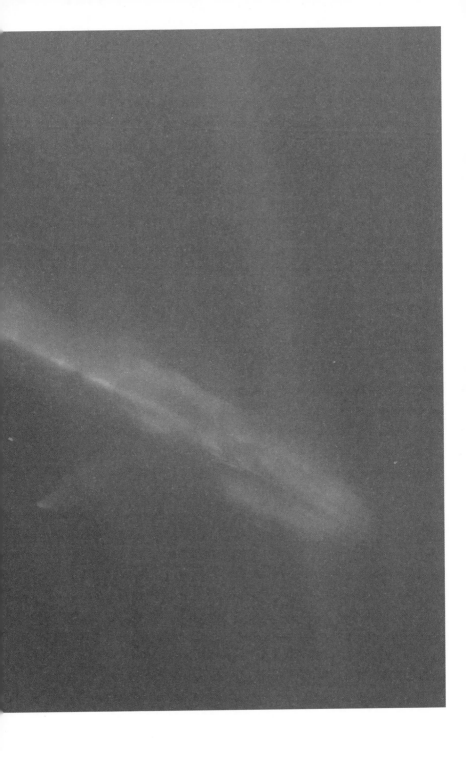

to have lived. It's taken me years of work to get here, and through the clear blue water and breath bubbles, I think of my father, poetically describing mackerel in August or dancing sandhoppers on the evening shore at Cuan Éamainn, Fenit Island.

I swim most days now if I can, sometimes with friends, often on my own. Summer is wonderful but winter is magical; sea swimming is a reflective, contemplative and at-times spiritual experience for me. I stop a few hundred metres out in the bay and lift my goggles to take in the winter Atlantic space – dark rolling swell approaches and raises me in the water, in the December sunset the sky is a darkly beautiful mix of deep blues, ever-changing with the monstrous grey clouds charging in from the ocean; they reveal the sun, its spells of tangerine magic casting glorious colour across sea and land, and my consciousness. I shiver to my core but inside, my mind is lit up.

A SENSE OF PLACE

PERHAPS WORDS TRIGGER a colour or pattern in your mind, as they do for me. Sunday is golden, autumn is a deep brown, and Clare is pale. Neither mountainous nor level, small, hilly, wet fields, innocuous, inoffensive. Our accent is flat, lacking the musicality of Cork or Kerry, the soft politeness of Donegal or gentle earnestness of Monaghan. I sometimes wonder what a person from Italy or Uzbekistan would make of us thinking we're different from other Irish people a few miles up or down the road. But sure enough we are, even if viewed only through the prism of a lifetime of observing each other.

I tease my Connemara friends how lucky they are to have Clare as their canvas, cliffs rising from the ocean like a great Jurassic fortress, protecting a landscape dramatically reaching out across the Burren, its miles of grey limestone appearing soft from that distance, curving into the rounded profile of the hills that rise above Black Head and into celestial skies, glowing in the soft light of winter days and summer evenings, hailing the disappearing sun, as a great warrior would a battle fought.

Like so many others, I left my home and Clare as much for the excitement of America as for the lure of casting off my small town 'stuff'. After many years of exile I returned to embrace this place, with the wisdom that the issues were in fact all mine.

It's a recurring story of immigrants, many men I've met and been, in The Bronx, Queens and Camden Town, but also ironically among American novelists, many from the Midwest, for some reason. Heartbroken by our loss of place, almost pitiably clinging to our identity of home, and with time frozen at the point of departure, rehashing again and again experiences of youth, neighbours, town bullies and lost love.

I'm sitting on an Aer Lingus jet facing west on a Shannon runway. I've just turned twenty years old. After long delays the monstrous thrust of the Rolls-Royce engines catapults us out towards the Atlantic and New York and, in my final glance through the window, I see my parents have waited in the rain. My father raises his right arm muscularly in salute, only knowing that I'm somewhere on board, the same arm that kept a one-year-old me eternally raised over his head in a ragged-eared photo somewhere in my attic, the same arm with which we pulled trammel nets together from freezing, early-morning seas. My mother maintains a loyal, dignified stillness. It would be another twenty years before she would tell me she cried in the car all the way back to Ennis.

Stop the plane, stop everything, get me off, my heart almost bursts with emotion. But it was too late. In his seminal album, *Frank's Wild Years*, Tom Waits sang, '*It was a train that took me away from here, but a train can't bring me home.*'

It was almost three years before I saw my parents again. I spent another eight years in North London and on sweltering summer Sundays I craved for the sea at Lahinch. Year after year.

The relief of gloriously chilly water and soft sand, salty faces and the easy banter of locals, 'Some day eh? Oh glorious, where else would you be.'

Nightmarish recollections flood back of three-hour funereal journeys under tarmac-melting sun to reach the stony 'beach' at Brighton with its murky brown water and piers of former glory rusting into the English Channel.

Back in Clare, I swim every day now, if I can.

~~~~~~

With so long an absence, the emigrant mind seeks to unfurl its psyche, almost concertina-like in recovering lost time on its return. I salute old school friends, who return confused gazes, I remember them clear as day, but they are distant. Time stops when you leave, but their experiences of years have diluted whatever they knew of you. And then there's the 'Sure look at your man, he's home now thinking he's great' brigade. I was more confused than bothered by them.

I used to run six miles in London, through Kentish Town, up the hill at Highgate, all the way to Hampstead across the Heath and back down the hill to my basement bedsit in Chalk Farm, six hard miles, but I loved it and my adage was to never stop. Now I run on the shore near White Strand, Miltown, and stop whenever I need to.

It's after sunset in November; a blackened sky bears down, merging with the ocean, and the only light is the breaking white water smashing into rock, a conversation hundreds of millions of years old. I've caught a shower, which in the north wind is perishing – I worry about my lungs breathing in the freezing wet air, I wonder if this is good for me, but mostly in my mind I'm free, floating across thoughts of exploring the ocean, of young love, lost friends, and time.

~~~~~~

I was snorkelling at Clahane near Liscannor in a low spring tide, many years ago now; kelp and thongweed filled the contracted water space like I'd never seen before, deep browns, golden browns, striking yellows – a dreamy secret garden you could explore in three dimensions and all reflected in the silvery, mirror-like underside of the water. It felt hallucinogenic and I marvelled at the idea of documenting this, of somehow articulating the experience.

And so my time exploring the underwater world took on new dimension, the discovery of vibrantly coloured life in the shallows along the Clare coast, reefs painted with pink encrusting algae, and myriad creatures and life forms, all dependent on, and in many cases killing, one another.

I stayed for hours every day, shivering in poorly fitting wetsuits.

I kayaked to Trá Bhán on the Great Blasket Island in early November 2008. I'd been trying to film mating seals for a couple of years along the Clare coast without success, but like so much in the natural world, it's about being in the right place. The journey

Clare's North Atlantic coast

is just over two miles from Coumeenole Beach on the mainland, a journey made thousands of times by the islanders, in all weathers, for births, weddings, funerals and perhaps on occasion a few drinks to smash the cabin fever of island life.

I break into Hank Williams' 'Your Cheatin' Heart' some-where in the Blasket Sound, safe from the listening ears of any other human. This truly feels like freedom, *'When tears come dow-www-n, like falling rain.'*

My cumbersome kayak clumsily surfs a wave onto the white sands of the island and as I tumble, I almost crash into a pair of copulating grey seals who are unperturbed by my presence. Christ, how many days I paddled the two miles to Seal Rock off Quilty to not see this.

At 2 pm the north-east-facing village of the island is in shade, and I realise with a sinking heart how long the winter days must have been for the island folks. My own people lived for 250 years on Fenit Island just thirty miles north of here. I stretch my visit until after sundown, in the knowledge that I 'know' my way home. In darkness and still a way out from Coumeenole I see disturbed water ahead; I could paddle around but I think, Sure, it'll be OK. It takes 45 minutes of pressure-paddling to cross a few hundred metres, at times I'm going backwards.

Later that night I study an admiralty chart on the wall of my B&B, Stromboli Rock it's called, and I can see the water is perhaps a metre deep on low spring tides, so there's likely 3 or 4 knots of tidal current running against you. I should have gone around.

~~~~~~

Many years later and just a few miles south-west of the Blaskets, I had another hallucinogenic experience. My lungs, now almost ten years older, had just enough gas to give me maybe a minute's breath-holding time down at ten metres depth trying to visually digest the extraordinary sight of competing Minke whales vigorously pumping their tail fins, building enough momentum to sweep in on shoals of sprat and sand eels. Their enormous mouths and throat pleats balloon open like parachutes and stall their eight-tonne bodies, now full of maybe ten tonnes of water and fish. The Minkes are here for the same reason the islanders were, the fertility of these waters. Unlike humpback whales, who seem to immediately squeeze the water out through their baleen (brush-like plates), the Minkes seem to hold it in for an age, and hang there almost inanimately, ghostly even, drifting on their momentum. I had tried for several years to film a Minke whale underwater, but they'd always been so elusive; now however, the bounty of shoals of fish has distracted them from my presence, much like breeding had done with the seals. I guess most life forms have two primary purposes, feeding and reproduction.

The Minkes, maybe eight or nine animals, come from every direction and I'm spinning my head, watching from as many angles as it will flex around to. You have to dive to really feel the three-dimensional nature of being in the water, because as a species almost everything we do is on the ground and in two dimensions. Can you imagine walking out into a busy traffic junction with small trucks not just crossing from every angle but also from above and underneath?

My dominant thoughts at the time were to shoot it well, and stay safe. Back on the boat the lads can hardly believe the video I play back for them; there was nothing to be seen from above water, was this always happening? Much of my fulfilment comes from watching these scenes later and articulating the event through film sequences. It transpires that this is the first time this behaviour has been documented anywhere and this section of my film will become an addition to what we know of these creatures and contribute to their conservation.

At the very end of November 2016 I followed clues I'd been monitoring for three years to an area 40 km west of Clare. Calm

Minke whale feeding, west of the Blasket Islands

seas at that time of year come with offshore winds from the east, bringing clear, crisp days that are sharply cold.

After a long day at sea in an open boat we are about to leave for home, but give it one last try, as you do, and follow signs of bird activity further offshore. We arrive to find thousands of seabirds screeching in primal screams, perhaps at the life-giving opportunity suddenly presented to them; gannets, any numbers of species of gulls. A great skua appears, looking for an easy kill of a distracted smaller bird. Then the ocean explodes: monstrous humpback whales lunging all around, eight of them, chasing shoals of sprat so big they blacken the sea. Common dolphins look midget-like beside the humpbacks, we panic, we literally don't know where to point our cameras because there's drama in every direction – after so many years, this long-sought nirvana moment appears right in front of me.

The whales rise out of the water, two at a time, monstrous mouths agape, sprat spilling over, and all of this before the Sun God celestially cheering and enriching the scene as if in some medieval religious painting. Water droplets sail into the air, backlit and painted by the glowing sunlight, itself after a journey of 90 million miles diffused magically through the filter of a few short miles of the Earth's atmosphere.

And then, after forty minutes, it was over, and all was quiet again.

We turn for home with the winter sun near tangerine on the horizon, now too low to colour the darkening sea, cold seeming to rise from its November mood. A shiver that begins at my neck shocks my body, but the land is now richly illuminated, the higher ground golden and Mount Callan's brown mosses appear as a welcoming warm hearth on the landscape. It seems as if all of the sea-facing windows of West Clare are responding, shining blood red, in a final parting ode to the failing sun.

I imagine within them, as in my own house, mothers cooking for homework-ridden school children, now noticing the temperature drop and stretching jumpers as if to keep the creeping cold at bay.

We've an hour's drive yet on the RIB (rigid inflatable boat) into a biting easterly airflow, but inside I'm illuminated, sad to be leaving the scenes we've just witnessed, but content to have documented what we have and yearning for the promise of warm tea in the hearth of a loving kitchen.

Humpback whales feeding west of Clare in November

Our work will help to understand and conserve the animals in this area, especially the whales. I'm overwhelmingly proud in a very parochial sense to have been able to find and film these scenes on my own doorstep in my own county. But they're not Clare whales, they're not Irish whales – the notion of human borders is absurd in this regard. Yet farther north, 1,300 Minke whales will be hunted and killed this year – possibly some of the same individuals I filmed in the Blaskets – because commercial whalers have convinced the Norwegian people that these so-called Norwegian whales are now sufficiently abundant to justify killing that many.

Academics talk about parochialism versus provincialism, one is good, the other not so much so, I never understood which or why.

On the scalding sidewalks of The Bronx, I met men from the villages of Clarecastle and Mullagh and Kilbaha, Clare men all and many, like me, struggling to survive in this threatening place. On Sundays many had had their fill of drink well before tea time: 'Éire Óg are in the county football final,' someone told me. I was proud of my former team mates. 'Townies will win nathin',' a Clarecastle man declared. 'My mother was from Clarecastle,' I told him. 'Ah fuck off,' he barked through drunken spittle.

In London I played football for the great Desmonds GAA club, made up mostly of Clare and Mayo men, we played a Galway crew, Naomh Mhuire in some or other final, a tough, tense match, I was out of my depth but never stopped trying and scored a point with a few minutes to go, to give us the lead. As if annoyed by such petulance, they went upfield and unleashed a bullet for the bottom corner – I can still see it, trying to glimpse the outcome through a field full of bodies, the ball in the net but from nowhere, the unyielding arm of the oldest man on the pitch, our goalie, cartwheeling into view almost in slow motion, and with one final athletic stretch, a fingertip touch saved the day. Oh he still had it, that boy.

Gasps spluttered from tired bodies, even from a couple of grudging Galwaymen. They scored the '45 and the ref blew it up for a draw. 'Go home ye Clare fuckers,' their big full back bellowed at us across the North London sky. We would if we could.

I had learnt Emily Lawless' poem 'Fontenoy, 1745' before it occurred to me that glorifying war was senseless and a hijacking of the art of poetry. But it still makes me cry:

Oh, little Corca Baiscinn, the wild, the bleak, the fair!
Oh, little stony pastures whose flowers are sweet, if rare!
Oh, rough the rude Atlantic, the thunderous, the wide,
Whose kiss is like a soldier's kiss which will not be denied!
The whole night long we dream of you and waking think
    we're there –
Vain dream, and foolish waking, we never shall see Clare

Almost three hundred years ago, these men from Corca Baiscinn, an area on Clare's Atlantic coast from Loop Head, north to Quilty, took what was likely the only option open to them to make a living, and joined foreign armies to fight wars. They probably weren't men at all, armies recruit teenagers for obvious reasons. Picture the vainglorious scene, West Clare men in French uniforms, on a blood-drenched Belgian battlefield, foot soldiers hopelessly under-equipped, in one final fling of their all-too-short young lives, they charge at a British cavalry regiment, pulling the enemy from their horses, bayonetting the falling men and winning the day for France. By the time they heard Irish accents from some of the British uniforms, it was too late.

Send us, ye western breezes, our full, our rightful share,
For Faith, and Fame, and Honour, and the ruined hearths
    of Clare.

Ken O'Sullivan

THE FENIT
REGATTA

I DOUBT THERE'S ANYONE ELSE ALIVE who remembers the 1932 Fenit regatta. Three-and-a-half decades before I was born, a few short years after Independence, a bloody civil war and in the midst of what my crying 70-year-old uncle Den called the 'hungry thirties', lifting his face square on to meet that of my father, who seemed to bow away in shame. Poverty brings shame, subsistence is the basest element of survival for any life form, and while we've no idea what animals feel, people's inability to feed themselves and their families brings on the most hopeless sense of inadequacy.

My father told me of walking four miles to school in the snow, barefoot. When he arrived the master looked down, and back up: 'Have you no shoes?' I believe it was the humiliation and not the excruciating pain that hurt most. Seven decades after the event, recounting the incident to me, his pain was ever-evident.

And then there's respectability: post-Famine Ireland underwent inordinate social change; the Catholic Church, already on the rise and building cathedrals and ornate churches at the height of the Famine on the pennies of impoverished paupers, sensed an opportunity for control. Victorian ideals, 'social order' as in hierarchical, stratified society as opposed to 'stability or harmony', gained what would become a deep-rooted emphasis within the people of Ireland, or at least some of them.

On my first sight of the great buildings at Westminster, London, I thought of the tiny smoky, windowless cottages of penal Ireland, the slavery and famine of India, and murderous deeds in any number of African countries. These were the magnificent, monstrous laurels of centuries of colonialism. For hundreds of years a popular notion permeated British writing and newspapers, that of the ignorant Irishman, semi-human, ape-like, illiterate and of course drunken.

I remember the 1932 Fenit regatta because I listened, as a child and later as a man, to countless recountings of the race by my father and his two brothers, between them the three-hand crew of our family's currach, or canoe as they call it in that part of Kerry. When a dozen or more verses of Milton or Shelley had been recited from seven-decade-old memories and the night was warming up, 'The year we won' would be dusted down off the top shelf and all three men would live again, the light of youth beaming through fiery eyes. Faces change, eyes remain the same.

The canoe wasn't just our family's main form of transport, it was the means by which they fished and supplemented their subsistence in the hungry thirties. My people, like many coastal folks, built their own boat, designed to suit local conditions, an enormous, skilful job with inherent responsibility for life or death at sea, but there must have been enormous pride in launching and fishing from your own hand-built boat.

Fenit Island

In recent years I met a wonderful man in his eighties, Paud Moriarty from Taulaght, a townland overlooking the lee side of Fenit Island. Paud recounted the sight of my grandmother and uncles arriving for Sunday mass in Churchill by canoe. 'Mass was timed to coincide with the high tide for the benefit of the island people arriving by canoe across the tidal estuary. On a spring tide, they'd get closer into the church, but on neaps they'd have a bit of a walk. Oh they could handle a canoe, those men,' he told me, squarely and earnestly.

At fifteen my father Billy was surely not old enough to row against men. Den was just seventeen and Jack, the eldest, nineteen, but handling a canoe was to them as handling a mustang

might be to a Cherokee Indian, or an icy mountain to a Sherpa. And so the opportunity to row against men from neighbouring villages, 'that crew from Ballyheigue', the Maharees men and the Joyces who somehow made it all the way from Connemara, and who, according to my father, would later row in the Olympics for Ireland, was too much of a rite of passage to miss.

My uncles Den, Jamie and Jack with my grand-uncle Dennis Sullivan visiting his home place on Fenit Island from Waterbury, Connecticut, sometime about 1950.
PHOTO: JOHN SULLIVAN USA

I don't know how long the race was, that kind of detail almost didn't seem important, just that you had to row out to and around a buoy and then race for home for 'all you're worth'. I do know that to reach the starting point at Fenit pier they rowed from the Dock, a small sheltered beach below their home in Baile Thuaigh, the north village, right around Fenit Island and into Fenit harbour, a sea journey of five miles.

The author on Inchiquin lake

Sadly I never rowed a canoe with my father – the last family one of my father's generation, built by him and my grandfather James Sullivan, a talented carpenter who also made his own fiddle and much more, was lost to the tide well before my time. But by the 1950s transport to mass and town had been taken over by a Volkswagen beetle – a wondrous machine to the islanders – albeit only when low tide allowed access across the tiny spit of tidal strand connecting Fenit Island to the mainland.

I grew up rowing my father around Inchiquin lake, him a little older by then and me, at about twelve, the perfect age to be pulling oars. He had built a wooden boat with just hand tools, as his father had done; someone named it *Vicky*. Once we arrived at the lake to discover the boat was missing and we searched and searched, my father so agitated, that my mother would later say, 'It was the first day his heart got bad.' We found *Vicky* smashed up on the far side of the lake. It's difficult to describe my father's reaction, not quite as losing a child, but something from deep within you, and maybe poorly understood. We left the scene in a darkness that remained over him for some time.

Then, perhaps a month later, he rose up and called us all to 'rig up the trailer, we're bringing that boat home somehow'. And somehow, we did. Weeks and months followed during which he whistled tunes with a pencil behind his ear, cut marine plywood, drilled precisely-placed holes with an old fashioned S-shaped hand drill, and followed the twist of brass screws into *Vicky's* new belly. How satisfying to watch a man at work with wood, metronomically sawing a straight line or smoothing a curve with a spokeshave, the scent of sawn and shaven timber mixed with that of Clan pipe tobacco.

Rowing is one of the most aerobically intensive of sports. As much of the power comes from your legs and lower back as it does from your arms and chest and like any endurance-based sport, the will to win is usually the deciding factor among those who already possess the basic skillsets, strengths and fitness.

Six or seven canoes took off on the starter's order; it was a fine enough summer's day, but there's always a south-westerly wind blowing up into Tralee Bay creating wind chop (small swells of waves maybe five or six yards apart). Halfway to the buoy my father and his brothers were already f****d, from there you survive on your 'will to win', they took the turn in second place, the Joyces flying it. Their canoe, my father would later discover, had been built specially for racing, with a tiny shallow draft – it sat way up in the water and held much less drag than the deeper working boats.

But the race wasn't over. This was their home place, their waters where their people lived and died, where they walked to school barefoot in the snow – aerobic pain is easy, barefoot humiliation perhaps less so. I can only tell you that when my father lifted his head desperately trying to catch his breath minutes after crossing the finish line and looked at the palms of his bleeding hands, he told me there was little or no skin left.

They rowed ashore to the cheering locals, their father, James Sullivan, carried shoulder-high by neighbours; the Olympian Joyces would have to wait another year. The prize money was one pound, which, as a neighbour boldly called out, bought 'twenty-four pints of Guinness' in those days and likely fed a family for a fortnight. But my father never drank much.

Almost fifty years later, in my early cycling races, I tried to conjure images of the '32 regatta. We used the word 'black' to describe when the pace was unbearable, when you felt you couldn't possibly go another yard, your lungs bursting with pain, and the only way to carry on was to somehow distract your mind. I didn't win a whole lot, but some years later in what would at fifteen be my greatest – if perhaps only – sporting achievement, I found myself in a pack of eighty cyclists at the All-Ireland road race in Mondello Park on a fine summer's day with light winds. It wasn't my first year here, but the seniors in our club had trained the hell out of us that summer, and we were strong. The pace was black all day, we raced 21 miles in 53 minutes, though that seems unbelievable now. About half way, my boyhood friend Cyril got away from the bunch, myself and the other Clare lads went to the front to try and slow the bunch down, not an easy thing, lots of effing and blinding from posh Dublin accents that clearly weren't practised at that kind of language, which kind of made me laugh, even in the blackness. The bunch swallowed Cyril who likely paid for his exertions. The pace never slowed until the last lap just before the Dunlop corner as we jostled for position, tucked in behind someone fast and timed our sprints. I felt I couldn't go on, and I was in a terrible position on the outside, coming around the corner, but I just put the head down and thought of skinless palms, and maybe twenty seconds later when I raised my head, I got one of the biggest frights of my young life to find myself in front, just ten metres from the line, sometimes what happens in a flash can take an age to recount … I'm sure I lost pace at realising where I was but recovered and threw a single arm into the air, perhaps it would draw the judges' eye to me, but either way I'd won by half a wheel. I went home to meet my father's gaze, square on.

SHALLOW DIVING

IF YOU LOOK YOU WILL SEE. Greater, more articulate men than I have probably put it a lot better, but the essence is the same. Exploring the shallow coastal waters off my native Co. Clare, I rarely come back from a dive without having seen or witnessed something new. Dive conditions can vary hugely in our wild temperate seas, but I find there is always something interesting to observe in the natural world.

In Clare we are blessed with a pristine Atlantic coastline, washed and smashed in equal measure by monster swells, many of which may have originated in Caribbean storms. On meeting the shallows, their energy is unleashed, its turbulence richly oxygenating the shallow waters and whipping up nutrients from the seabed. This creates a fertile, abundant ecosystem, not to mention some of the best surfing waves on the planet. On the stretch of coastline from Spanish Point to Lahinch, the same reefs that can give perfect, barrelly waves are also home to an abundance of marine life.

If, of course, you can get into the water there.

It's June and I've waited endlessly for the glassy seas needed to dive one of these reefs on the outside of a small rocky outcrop known locally as Green Island. Arriving to the shore just after

5 am, close to midsummer's day, the sun peeks over the hills for the first time, almost at its most easterly point of the year.

It's not that I'm a natural early riser, just that these inter-tidal reefs can only be dived at high tide and preferably the extra depth of spring tides with water five metres deeper than it would be at low water. From a photography perspective, we're looking for a day with no swell or wind and preferably some sunlight with a spring tide – but these conditions might coincide about ten times a year. There is not a day when there isn't some white water breaking over these reefs, and in this place I have filmed dramatic swells crashing over and sculpting the sandstone rock features, punishing the soft earth of the upper shore. But today these shallow reefs are placid and almost spiritually calm.

I first explored these reefs while snorkelling in early summer some years ago and vowed to return with my dive gear and camera. Although they are close to shore, access is a two-kilometre walk from the nearest road, which would mean lugging dive gear, camera, housing, tripod and the 16 kg of lead weights I wear for shallow-water filming, so I elect instead to load the lot onto a kayak at a road-access point a couple of kilometres to the south, and paddle there. The kayak can be stored on the small rocky island and I can slip into the water right on the reefs with my dive gear. Sounds simple, but it's a lot of gear.

Three trips from car to shore, and I push off through a channel maybe a couple of metres wide, where I've seen winter waves funnel and smash lumps off the soft cliffs. But not today. Paddling in the 6mm-dive wetsuit is immediately sweltering, I scoop seawater in at the neck to cool down, and even stop for a short dip on the way.

A lobster fisherman is checking his pots a few hundred metres offshore, his vibrantly red trawler almost perfectly reflected on the glassy, windless sea. Beyond, a layer of sea fog is smudged across the northern side of Liscannor Bay, its outline visible at both ends, giving it the feel of a bank of fog. Paddling through the shallows I can see golden kelp below, its long summer fronds swaying gently, periodically revealing swathes of pink algae along the rocky shallows. There is a surreal, almost intimate beauty in the early summer morning.

I've made this trip many times now, and the habit is well established. I drag the kayak laden with dive and camera gear well up onto the tiny island, don dive gear, weights, mask, check the camera housing, take a couple of shots to make sure all's well with the camera, sit at the water's edge and recall the only two words of Swahili I learned in Africa, *Hakuna Matata* (no problem). I always, always chill before a dive. Fins on, I slip into the midsummer sea and welcome the refreshing water.

~~~~~~

My first enquiry is always about the state of the water and today visibility and light are pristine. God, the relief – this is my twelfth dive here and while I've always seen the potential, it can be agonisingly difficult documenting this wonderful world if conditions aren't in your favour.

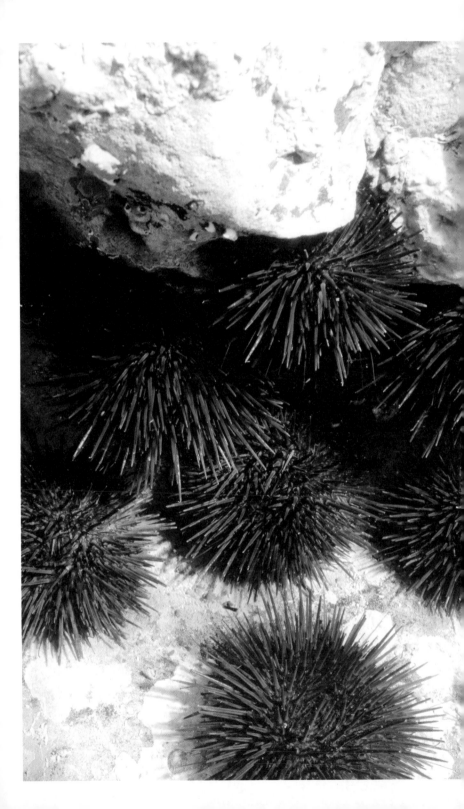

Lazily diving around the reefs you could lose yourself exploring and examining its vibrant life forms. Scuba diving is like flying. A slight fin kick and you glide as if in slow flight, breathe out and you descend a little with the buoyancy change, welcoming the dark. Breathe in and you rise in the water towards the light. Sun rays radiate upliftingly through the shallows, illuminating the creatures and their flamboyant hues, a dance between light and colour, as old as the sun.

There are a multitude of seaweed species here, browns, greens and reds, forests of new-season kelp, with golden-brown blades, their stems covered with eagle-like claws wonderfully known as 'holdfast', which they do through the wildest of storms. I meet walls of aptly-named thongweed so thick they form a jail-like barrier from reef to sea surface, but with a gentle push, you can easily glide through. I love to grasp it in my hands and as it slides through my fingers feel the natural oils, the same ones that enrich expensive cosmetics craved by city folk in a desperate reach out for an elemental connection with nature.

Trying to film this, however, intrudes on my dream state – nonetheless, what I can document will be something to take away with me and recount to others.

The reefs are smothered in pink encrusting algae, giving them an almost psychedelic look, and pockmarked with hundreds of

OPPOSITE: *Purple urchins on a shallow reef*

FOLLOWING SPREAD: *Shallow reef with holes created by purple urchins, some now occupied by anemones, with barnacles, mussels, whelks, weed all living along the reef.*

Whelks feeding on mussels

tennis ball-sized holes ground out over thousands of years by purple urchins seeking shelter. Although sadly now classified as locally extinct due to overfishing in the 1980s, they are abundant here, though many of their holes have become occupied by vibrantly-coloured anemones squatting for shelter.

Higher up the reef carpets of acorn barnacles compete with common mussels and limpets for rock space. Whelks are abundant in their conical shells with growth lines weaving through colours from dark crimson at the pointed end to a brilliant white at the opening. They use tentacles to expeditiously feel their way around until their bodies ooze from their shells out over their favourite prey, acorn barnacles and mussels. The whelks bore holes into the immobile mussels using a tiny razor-like tongue covered in a kind of acidic saliva. They then insert toxins through this hole to paralyse the unfortunate creatures, whose muscles relax, causing its shell to open, at which point the whelk eats the soft body part of the mussel.

Buddhists say everything is connected.

Mussels occasionally respond with their only defence, which is to spin byssal threads; acting in groups, they spin and weave enough threads to tie up their predator. If you look through any mussel beds along the intertidal area you will see occasional empty whelk shells tied by many strands to a mussel colony, the hapless whelk long dead and its carcass likely eaten by another creature of this marvellous ecosystem, the hermit crab. These sprightly little creatures are born without a shell, but learn to inherit the empty shells of other creatures such as whelks, or in this case, eat the remains and then move in. Today I can see a hermit crab in one such shell, scavenging on the scraps of a mussel which had been mostly eaten by a whelk. Other molluscs are then feeding on the light green algae on the outside of the whelk shell, though the hermit crab's sudden comic movements are testing their grip.

I glide down into slightly deeper waters and spot fattened starfish devouring mussel colonies. In the past I've set the camera on a tripod here and filmed a time-lapse over a few hours. Speeded up, it looks a gooey, ghoulish other-worldly scene as the starfish slither across the mussels, gorging themselves.

Nudibranch eating a beadlet anemone

A nudibranch (sea slug) straddles an unfortunate beadlet anemone, already paralysed by the slug's deadly toxins, albeit only in this macroworld. The dull purple pigment from previously digested anemones is visible on the nudibranch's skin; it has reused this, but even more amazingly, the nudibranch can absorb the anemone's own toxins without any reaction and store them for reuse against other anemones and other prey, an ingenious example of evolutionary adaptation.

Everything is connected.

Half a century before my time here, there was a legendary local angler named Jack Shine who used to climb out to the edge of

Green Island at low tide, and while standing on these very reefs where I now dive, Jack would catch porbeagle sharks. In fact he caught porbeagles up to around 145 pounds. Catching sharks from the shore was almost globally unique at that time, in fact, outside of Florida and Australia, Green Island, Co. Clare was the first place in the world where an angler dared to entice and catch sharks from the shore. Sadly, Jack Shine had passed on before my time here, but he was a true legend in many ways, and all across Ireland and the UK, he's still revered by serious anglers. My neighbours recall Jack as a genial, thoughtful man, a hugely talented musician; he played the clarinet and accordion and drove a motorcycle with a sidecar. Jack also owned a 16mm film camera and filmed scenes of local people and farming activities from the 1950s onwards. True innovators express themselves in many ways.

Porbeagles are strikingly similar in appearance to their cousins, the great white. They grow on average to about two and a half metres, but the Irish catch record for a porbeagle is 365 pounds (161kg). In all my years diving here, I dream of encountering a porbeagle shark underwater, and whenever I sense a shadow or unexplained movement through the darkness of the water, I turn in hope. One day my time will come.

For now I'm trying to document much of this world with its smaller creatures, working with macro photography, which is extreme close-up photography of small subjects. Using a 35mm sensor camera and lenses like these means focusing is super-critical where your depth of field, i.e. the lateral amount of your subject which can be in focus, may be as little as 3 to

4 mm, so a tripod is an absolute necessity. But even on the calmest, glassiest day, there is wave surge in water this shallow and while being thrown back and forth, I try to focus my own eye on the viewfinder and set the camera focus as I'm swept a metre either side of the camera – didn't get it this time, I'll try on the way back … and so it goes until there's a break in the swell.

Many times a stronger set of waves will knock over the tripod, so you have to always have a hand ready, and at least once in every session I lose patience and blow off. 'I just can't do this, it's impossible.' Just as well the creatures can't hear me, but maybe the release helps and I'm always back moments later, trying again. In one such moment I rose to the surface to get some relief, only to discover my kayak has drifted away in the rising tide. After removing my dive gear and packing all the kit on a high-up rock, I find the kayak after a five or six-hundred-metre swim, not an easy feat in a bulky scuba dive suit with limited arm movement.

Yes there's a glaring contradiction here between enjoying the beauty of this natural world and my own striving in attempting to document it, but I guess that's for me to figure out.

THE ISLANDER'S DANCE

In the long slow weeks of midwinter
Before the daylight turns to face another year
And nights begin, before the day has even spun
The islanders itch for mainland sun

Walk the same stretch of ragged shore
Each day, through rock pools, searching, combing for
Seaborne gifts from sunken ships
Remembered lore of whiskey barrels
And cotton, timber and fragrant jars
Tucked away before bailiff eyes, and informer breath
Could steal them away from the islander hearth

Lobsters dance the full moon night
And the islanders too
Take flight
East, to the mainland, on currachs bare
Gliding, giddy, sailing towards
Whiskey scent, the porter barrel
Tobacco smoke and maidens' mirth.
The brush dance, ancient madness, handed down

And in time, the songs and lore of yore
Fill the air, and free the ghosts
And the room fills and bursts
With the wonder and streams of human dreams
And fairy's tunes and verse,
From other worlds

Then fluid oars on ocean rhythm
Westwards across glassy seas they sing
Of nets full and battles dark
Of island men at Gettysburg
And Massachusetts and North London
Days of youth and islands lost

The full moon night, the angry sea
Forgives such flight, this once
And after dance
The lobster sleeps
Released, tonight.

THE LIFE OF A
FILM-MAKER

MEGAPTERA NOVAEANGLIAE, literally big-winged New Englander, is the scientific name for the humpback whale, in reference to the animal's giant pectoral fins, which can grow to five metres in length. The name was likely first described in New England, where newly-landed Europeans developed commercial whaling into a huge industry from the 1700s onwards, though Native American peoples hunted whales long before then along the north-east coast of the US.

Humpbacks are perhaps one of the most charismatic of whales, though that observation is a human indulgence. I'm not convinced dolphins or other animals have a preference between whale species, but humpbacks' curiosity for boats, swimmers and other 'strange' forms in the ocean, and their habit of breaching clear out of the water have nonetheless endeared them to us.

But these are amazing animals, they have the longest known migration route of any mammal, with several humpbacks recorded swimming from Bear Island in Northern Norway to the Cape Verde islands off West Africa, a sea journey of more than 7,000 km.

From summer to midwinter, they feed on herring, sprat and any other fish they can locate in northern latitudes from Greenland to Iceland to Norway to Ireland etc. and then migrate south to the tropics to meet other humpbacks of the opposite sex and breed and give birth before making the reverse journey north; this period may span up to five months, during which time the animals don't feed and so must live off their fat reserves.

South of the equator, the exact opposite occurs, with southern humpback whales, a distinct sub-species, feeding in southern latitudes before migrating north to the tropics towards the equator.

~~~~~~~

The Irish Whale & Dolphin Group (IWDG), under Dr Simon Berrow has been studying humpback whales in Ireland for a long time. There were no recorded sightings of humpbacks here for perhaps fifty years, then in 1999 two swam up to the Kinsale gas rigs and lolled at the surface long enough for one of the workers to take some video footage. By 2011 Simon and Pádraig Whooley, IWDG Sightings Officer, had collected photographic identification of about twenty individual humpbacks in Ireland, but where they went to breed remained unknown, despite ten years of search efforts. Locating their breeding grounds would facilitate trying to have the animals protected in that area and perhaps other areas between there and their feeding grounds.

In spring 2011 I accompanied Conor Ryan, a brilliant young scientist from Cobh, to the Cape Verde islands, 500 km west of Senegal and Mauritania. Old whaling records from Yankee whalers had indicated the possibility of the islands being used by breeding humpbacks, but very little was known. Simon and his colleagues had even sailed to Cape Verde from Ireland in 2003, just a paltry 4,000 km, and had encountered humpbacks, but Cape Verde is an archipelago of ten islands, some, hundreds of kilometres apart, and the trade winds, so named for the trade they facilitated to the new world of the Americas, race through here, tearing up the sea and so searching for whales is extremely challenging.

Most forms of successful research go through iterations or even generations of work, each building on the previous, before substantial breakthroughs. By 2011 Conor Ryan had decided to narrow the search to the island of Boa Vista where there were definite humpback sightings each spring. Having spent his youth around boats and the sea, Conor decided that a small mobile vessel was the best platform to approach and track these large fast-moving whales. Up to that point there had been just a few photographs of humpbacks from the islands and one biopsy sample. Using a crossbow, scientists fire a dart with an empty tubular tip about five millimetres thick, at the whales, which penetrates perhaps a couple of centimetres into the skin and blubber before bouncing back courtesy of a rubberised bung on the dart. The dart is collected from the water and these biopsy samples contain invaluable information about the whales. For example, Conor was able to study what the whales had been feeding on, by matching markers in their skin to those of known fish such as sprat and herring. He was also hoping to extract DNA and analyse genetic information to ascertain if the humpbacks in Cape Verde were likely related to the humpbacks encountered around Ireland.

Breaching humpback, Cape Verde. PHOTO: CONOR RYAN

DNA is a very powerful tool.

By mid-April 2011 Conor was already steaming ahead and discovering more and more humpbacks around Boa Vista. We spent eight to ten hours at sea every day on a tiny four-metre RIB, perhaps a quarter of the length of some of the humpbacks we were chasing. The trade winds blow west, away from Cape Verde, and more than once I wondered of the consequences of the single engine failing on this tiny boat … The next stop was

the Caribbean, 4,000 km to the west, drifting at maybe 50 km per day; you might make landfall in eighty days, though that's not accounting for the doldrums, the no-wind areas, and we only had enough water to last maybe a few days at any rate. There's no coast guard in Cape Verde and our radio might have worked for 20 km to call someone to help us, if anyone was listening ... but Conor was very motivated, and we ploughed on.

I'd never been so close to humpbacks. We tracked alongside and within a few metres of some animals; the females were enormous, often one and a half to two metres longer than the males. They'd sometimes rise alongside the RIB, Conor would be waiting with his crossbow, some animals might flinch when hit, or occasionally give a loud trumpet-like exhalation telling us they're not happy with something, but mostly they didn't react to the dart.

Pedrin López Suárez, a brilliant and vastly experienced Spanish marine researcher based in Boa Vista, had facilitated Conor

Filming a breaching humpback, nervously, off Boa Vista, Cape Verde, 2011. PHOTO: PEDRIN LÓPEZ SUÁREZ

with accommodation, the RIB and crucial local knowledge. As whales rose, Conor and Pedrin would often recognise the animal individually by the shape of its dorsal fin, competing with each other to get the animal's name or number out first. 'Pedrin, it's Scar and look – he has a girlfriend.' 'Yes Conor, and she's the same female we saw three years ago.' This went on day after scaldingly hot sunny day. Pedrin told me he had worked with a pod of 150

bottlenose dolphins in the Gulf of Mexico and could recognise every individual animal by the shape of its dorsal fin.

After about a week, from a distance, we spot huge splashes and commotion in the sea, in among whale blows. We arrive to witness at least five humpbacks lunging aggressively, almost brutally, at each other. They rise out of the sea with deafening blows, and dive directly at the other animals. Conor and Pedrin figure out that this is a mother and young calf and two males who appear to be competing for breeding access to the female – but she already has an 'escort', a male humpback who tends to the mother and calf and protects them from interlopers, though as with many things in nature, we're still not sure if this male is a breeding partner.

For forty-five minutes the males lunge at each other, or try to get between the mother and her calf, but the escort male defends them and the female is bigger and more powerful, and also rises from the sea combatively charging at the interlopers. It is a frightening, primal display but likely something that has occurred for the 50 million or so years that these animals have existed in this form. In truth it's almost impossible to define exactly what is occurring other than to say that the males were clearly seeking to make an impression.

And then, suddenly, it's over. The mother, calf and escort disappear, and, as if defeated, the two males rise calmly to the surface and just loll there in the sun, breathing ever more slowly.

I look at Conor and we know this is my chance, 'It's up to you,' he says, and without thinking further, I'm in the water, gently finning towards the animals with my camera. Their size alone is terrifying, more so as they turn their eye and swim towards me, 35 tonnes, the weight of six elephants and size of a double decker bus.

I hang in the blue water about ten metres from the two whales, who are gently moving in a direction perpendicular to mine. One turns to face me and with the slightest movement of its giant tail fin, floats right up to within a few metres, its eye moving, sizing me up, as we'd say in rural speak. I'm six foot four, but I've never felt so small in all my life, as this 45-foot (15-metre) prehistoric animal drifts in to investigate the odd-shaped life form of a submerged human. I keep the camera rolling and try to make the most of the opportunity and within a minute or so, the animal fins again, twisting its body around, away from me, tucking in its pectoral fin to avoid a collision, and then it's gone. A bit like falling in love, I told my wife on the phone later – 'really'!

~~~~~~~

With his unquenchable passion for documenting the natural world, Conor managed to document thirty-seven individual humpback whales using photographic ID during his six-week trip to Cape Verde, getting biopsy samples from twenty-eight individual animals, and clearly establishing that Cape Verde was and remains a breeding area for these animals. Of the estimated 11,600 humpback whales across the North Atlantic, Conor worked out that there were just 260 using the Cape Verde islands as a breeding grounds. Our current knowledge is that almost all

A happy day at sea off Cape Verde 2012. PHOTO: GEORGE KARBUS

other humpbacks use the Caribbean breeding grounds, hence the
Cape Verde animals are hugely important and their protection
is critical.

I had been exhausted when I went to Cape Verde after spending two years producing a six-part Irish ocean wildlife series, the
first ever on Irish TV; it was a mammoth task, but we delivered a
unique series that was extremely well received. I came back from
Cape Verde though, greatly empowered and energised to try and
document the story of humpbacks in the North Atlantic and especially the search for the breeding grounds of ones seen in Ireland
as well as all the other compelling facets to Conor's research work.

Showing some local lads a video of humpback whales underwater, Boa Vista, Cape Verde. PHOTO: GEORGE KARBUS

I felt this was a unique and powerful story for a documentary film, combining groundbreaking research collaboratively with blue-chip cinematography and paying homage to the ancient maritime heritage of the Cape Verde islands and Ireland's Atlantic coast. I even had a name, *Whale Watcher.*

Cape Verde's people fascinated me; they were colourful and unique, living in this tiny republic out in the Atlantic. Women arrived early to fish markets with huge basins of fish balanced on their heads, they teased me when I asked to take photos, but I smiled my way to permission. Fishing was rudimentary but artisan; often we'd meet a lone fisherman in a small, colourful wooden

Cape Verde woman at fish market in Sal Rei, Boa Vista island

boat maybe twenty miles offshore, smiling and helpful. '*Balena, balena?*' we'd call out and he'd invariably point in the direction where he'd last seen a humpback.

There were likely no indigenous peoples on Cape Verde before its 15th-century Portuguese colonisation. There's darkness within its past: it became a successful slave-trading station where, for three centuries, agents sold humans stolen from Africa to be transported to the Caribbean for a life of drudgery.

But something was different on Cape Verde. Slaves who were retained on the islands could earn their freedom after years of work; many mixed and had families with 'free people' and so Portuguese, Mauritanian and Senegalese people gave birth to a unique and new Creole culture. The music, oh the music, fusions of African and Portuguese rhythms, melody and instrumentation, to which Cape Verdeans dance expressively with their athletic bodies in a way that my gangly Irish frame could admire but best not attempt. There is a unique Cape Verdean singing style called 'Morné', similar and possibly derived from the Portuguese Fadó style of mournful singing, usually practised by women. It's a breathtaking, heart-stopping, eloquent expression of human pain and suffering.

Yankee whalers arrived here in the 18th century, always in need of deck hands, and in the Cape Verdeans they found hardy, seafaring, muscular young men. They hunted whales here, but the population was probably small and so the stock appears to have collapsed relatively quickly.

Unless you're a sailor, it seems a geographically puzzling fact that, when sailing from New England to the Pacific Ocean, the American whalers would first sail southwest to the Azores, then south on to Cape Verde where they'd pick up the trade winds that would then bring them back southeast to Cape Horn in southern Chile's Tierra del Fuego archipelago, where some of the world's stormiest waters mean that it could take up to two months to round the Horn on into the Pacific.

But whalers knew what they were about and in a certain sense, they actually chartered global trade, at least in the modern age, the lure of whale oil and its financial bounty drawing them across the globe to places where they forged trading and cultural links, which still endure today. I find it fascinating that many thousands of Cape Verdeans stayed with the Yankee whalers and settled in

Fisherman casting a hand net in the town of Sal Rei, Boa Vista

New England, many of them in New Bedford, Massachusetts, perhaps the home of American whaling, although Cape Cod's Nantucketers would strongly disagree. In fact, there are almost as many Cape Verdeans in Massachusetts as there are on Cape Verde.

There is a lovely parallel here in that many of the people formerly of the Blasket Islands, a place where humpback whales migrate to feed on rich fish stocks, went to settle in Springfield, Massachusetts, less than a hundred miles from New Bedford. I guess though, these are just stories of human migration, and as someone who lived abroad for thirteen years, I well understand how folks emigrate to places where they have friends and relatives, and this is how communities form.

~~~~~~

I spent all of the rest of 2011 and into 2012 researching this film project, working and reworking treatments, proposals and promo videos for funders and broadcasters. For the winter months when humpbacks were feeding off the south coast, we pulled our RIB behind my underpowered ageing car all across the country, in search of humpbacks. We often went to Kilmore Quay in Wexford, a five-and-a-half-hour drive in the darkness of December and January. I still hadn't managed to raise any funding, but carried on believing I'd try even harder and the big break was just around the corner.

I'd stay in Wexford the night before so as to launch the boat at sunrise, which at that time of year is 8.30 am. With sunset just after 4pm, we'd have just six hours at sea, allowing for a safety hour in case of trouble on the way home. I couldn't afford a B&B for the second night and would drive back to Clare after we'd recovered the boat and cleaned up. I couldn't even pay for a B&B for our boat-driver Richard Creagh, a young marine biologist hugely enthusiastic about whales and nature in Ireland, though I was at least able to give him a wage. I told him to sleep at home in Cork and we'd wait for him to make the two-hour journey in the morning, but he knew the days were short and getting to sea at sunrise was essential, so he would sleep in his jeep on the pier at Kilmore Quay, I felt truly awful at not being able to pay for a bed for him, and I still do, but I simply didn't have the money.

The 2008 financial crisis and ensuing deep recession left our production company devastated. I would hear people complain that their salaries had dropped by 10 or 15 per cent with tax increases, but like many small businesses, our income dropped to more or less zero.

Still we carried on, as you must. Without any resources other than me and my camera, it was proving intensely difficult to get enough video footage of whales in our winter seas, to make a film, and this was the age before drones. Ireland is one of the most difficult places in the world to film whales. There are very few animals in a vast area, seas are rough, water clarity is poor and feeding whales are usually moving. People are used to beautiful, perfectly stable, crystal-clear whale scenes from BBC films, but there's a reason why they don't choose Irish waters to film whales, at least not underwater.

My friend, the photographer George Karbus, who spent many a year on the RIB with me searching for whales, often just the two of us and even sharing the driving, called me once on his return from Hawaii: 'Ken, it's so easy there, man, there must be thirty whales in this tiny bay.'

~~~~~

In the spring of 2012 I returned to Cape Verde with Conor who had stayed supportive of my efforts all through. Conor managed to get a further twenty-one whale biopsy samples, getting within the range of fifty samples, which is the magic sample size needed for genetics research. The story just got better.

Conor completed his research with some extraordinary results. He carried out genetic analysis on almost fifty humpbacks around Cape Verde and several more in Ireland: sadly the results showed there was no match between the animals encountered in these areas, but crucially he confirmed that the Cape Verde stock was genetically distinct from other North Atlantic humpback whales, making them a subpopulation and hence hugely important to conserve.

Conor found worrying residues of chemicals such as DDT and PCBs in the animals' blubber. DDT was a 'wonder drug', an organochloride pesticide, actually used to treat malaria and typhus in troops in World War II and later used widely both in agriculture and as a household pesticide. It was another in a long line of supposed cure-all magic solutions, except it was eventually discovered – or perhaps it's more correct to say it was eventually admitted – that it did enormous environmental harm particularly to wildlife and birds but was also carcinogenic to humans and possibly other creatures. DDT is washed off the land into rivers and the sea and lodges in the fatty cells of marine creatures, so large fatty animals like whales were worst affected; being at the top of the food chain, the chemicals from the smaller animals they eat accumulate in their blubber, and as this is converted into milk fat for their calves, the toxic load is passed on between generations.

Crucially, Conor's thesis was later cited by the International Whaling Commission when they were called as an expert witness in the landmark international court case taken by the Australian and New Zealand governments, which brought an end to Japanese

Dr Conor Ryan taking whale biopsy samples off the Wexford coast aboard Celtic Mist

commercial whaling in the Antarctic on the basis that a single biopsy sample collected with a dart could tell you everything you needed to know scientifically about a whale, and so the notion of killing whales for science was a complete misnomer and indeed a scientific fraud. The Japanese 'research' programme was shut down by court order, but dispiritingly, the Japanese found a loophole and just began a 'different' research programme. This was again challenged legally, and at time of writing, Japan has decided to leave the International Whaling Commission and cease whaling in the Southern Ocean. However, they will expand whaling within their own waters. Oh the folly of humanity.

In my time as a natural history film-maker, I've repeatedly come across fervent individuals carrying out groundbreaking and hugely important conservation research, be it with whales, dolphins, sharks, skates, birds etc. I struggle to understand why more of this kind of work isn't being done by institutions of the state, as it is in other countries, even and indeed especially Northern Ireland and the rest of the UK. Yes, of course much research and conservation work is done, but clearly not nearly enough: I've always done my best to work collaboratively with researchers, institutions, government bodies and so forth to achieve our common goals of education, awareness and conservation, and for 98 per cent of the time this has been hugely positive.

I guess if we struggle to deliver a functioning health service, one could ask why spend money and resources on the natural world; but there are myriad reasons why we should, not least of which is our obligations to conserve and protect the billions of other species on our planet and the importance of the natural world to our own health and well-being.

～～～～～

I carried on through another winter of trying to film humpback whales in Ireland without any funding and chasing broadcasters and film distributors without success.

On one particular day we went to sea off Wexford looking for whales: two fin whales were swimming slowly enough to be approachable, and after several failed efforts, Conor spotted one swimming right at the boat and shouted 'Quick, quick get in!' and I did what a cameraman, but most especially an underwater cameraman, should never do – I rushed. Jumping into the water, I called out to Conor to pass me the camera housing. As I took it from him while turning to face the whale, one of our hands caught the latch and the housing opened, the lid fell to the depths and the camera and lens inside were flooded and destroyed. A moment later, the fin whale swam past, its eye glancing up at me. It would be another six years before I got close enough again to film a fin whale in the water. The financial loss of nearly €5,000 I needed like a hole in the head.

Later that same day we were eating our lunch on a flat calm sea about twelve miles offshore when a wave of water appeared from nowhere, slapped into the RIB and filled the boat with a foot of seawater; I just about got my dry camera off the floor to avoid damage, literally my last piece of film-making equipment left. We were flabbergasted: where had this wave come from? Another vessel, a twin-hulled catamaran whale-watching boat had done a 180-degree manoeuvre at high speed close by and whipped up the water, which slowly and quietly made its way to us.

Back home, I managed to fix up a very old standard definition camera and housing and continued using that to film in the water. I'd now spent two years trying to make this documentary, I felt we'd been close at times to getting funding, but the reality was I'd been refused by seventeen broadcasters in fourteen countries and by a list of state agencies whom I really felt could have helped as they were doing little or no cetacean conservation research at what was a vital period in the recovery of humpback whale numbers. The body responsible for issuing our whale-filming permit had withheld it for almost two months, giving no reason, and by the time they finally issued it in late January, the humpbacks had all left Ireland for their breeding grounds. I asked the official in the department if he was aware that we were the only people actually taking the trouble to apply for the permits. I'd met TV news crews at sea, and lots of other boats with documentary crews and professional photographers, and almost none was even aware a permit was required. When I put this to the official, he responded that what we were doing was a 'commercial' interest whereas TV news crews were considered a public service. He later emailed me stating he wished to withdraw this comment.

Sometime in 2012 I was pulling the RIB to West Cork in my now 15-year-old Volkswagen. We could only use harbours with low-gradient slipways, which in reality meant most slipways were inaccessible to us, as the car wasn't able to recover the RIB and trailer up steep slips. Things were by now financially disastrous, I struggled to even pay for diesel and at times I must have driven home on fumes. I was racking my brains for hours on that drive, trying to think of a way to get funding.

At some point on the journey a wave of emotion came over me and I burst into tears. I pulled the car over and just cried for 20 minutes, why was this so hard, why was no one helping me, how was I going to support my family. Even broadcasters for whom we'd killed ourselves working and delivering quality documentaries shunned all our applications.

After two years, I was broke, exhausted and I hadn't made the film.

My only realistic option was to go to Australia, I knew someone who had contacts in mining and there was work driving machines. I shuddered at the thought, but I would go if I had to.

I had been knocking on RTÉ's and many other doors for years at that point without success, but finally, when it seemed there was no other opportunity to make a living, never mind a documentary about whales, a chink of light appeared: RTÉ expressed interest in an ocean wildlife series. But natural history documentaries need multiple funders, more so in the era of declining broadcaster revenue.

I worked in what you might term the 'private sector' and ran my own business for many years and I understand that businesses must of course be commercially viable and generate enough income to justify investment. But making TV documentaries, especially natural history ones, is not commercially viable in our world. The likes of the BBC's *Blue Planet*, for example, is financed by national broadcasters based on public money in four or five countries with combined populations of hundreds of millions of viewers and likely budgets of €1.5–2 million per TV hour. RTÉ simply couldn't compete with those budgets, but Irish TV viewers expect broadly similar standards. We therefore have to seek public financing from other areas such as the TV licence fee and government departments and initiatives.

Mícheál Ó Cinnéide was a director at the Environmental Protection Agency (EPA), a West Kerry man with island heritage like myself, and an impressive track record of achievement in environmentalism and conservation in Ireland. Mícheál had come to some of our film screenings and always participated in our audience Q&As afterwards, which were invariably lively and conservation-focused. I called him in late 2012 and asked if the EPA might be able to assist with funding. Finally, after procedures and applications, the EPA became the first people to say yes to supporting any our projects in almost three years.

I do ponder the notion of parallel lives, so easily things could be different for any of us.

With the EPA's support we had increased credibility. RTÉ backed us to go forward to the Broadcasting Authority of Ireland to apply for funding from a portion of the TV licence fee, and although it would be almost another full year, we eventually got the series funded and went on to produce a four-part series on life in the shallow waters around Ireland delivered in 2014. The project was hugely well received and highlighted many key environmental and marine conservation issues.

I wasn't able to make the humpback film, and it would be several more years before I was able to tell any part of the story of humpbacks in Irish waters, but I did eventually manage to document several things for the first time, such as their feeding behaviour underwater and local feeding patterns in Ireland, which have added to what we know of these animals and how we can try to protect them.

Conor's work was rightly lauded in scientific circles although he would humbly make the point that it built on the work of many others before him – rarely does one person make such a difference.

I am still greatly saddened not to have been able to tell his story.

CLUB HURLER

Long ago he realised
The adorations of masses
Were for men more silken-skilled than he
On garland days.

Tuesday nights on wet March muck
When only the few showed
For training
Were his fare now
Timber and torn fingers
And playin' out of his skin
Would be just enough
To keep him from Junior B.

The jersey, old but clean, inherited from proud men
Would be his
For a while.
And on Saturday evenings
Over in the park
Or sodden country pitches
Only grinding of teeth and fits
Of anger would be enough
To reach the summit of ordinariness.

CILL STIFFIAN STORM

Somewhere in a cloud between need and stress my judgement waned. Cill Stiffian is a big lumpy reef that runs across the outer edge of Liscannor Bay, five or six miles out from Lahinch. As its boulders rise to lurk just a metre below the surface at low tide, breaking white water is the only betrayal of its presence. It's even hard to say where it is because that depends on where you're looking from. Standing on Lahinch beach, you'd swear it was in the middle of the bay, but from the south side you'd think it was right up north. It's all about perspective.

Cill Stiffian, Stephen's Church, the old people have a rhyme about it which I can't remember but the last line says if you see it, you're about to die. The lost city of Cill Stiffian is supposed to have been a village that sank in a well-documented sixth-century tsunami that hit the Clare coast. Legend has it there is a key hidden somewhere up Mount Callan which, if you can find and dip in the sea, will allow Cill Stiffian to rise again, led by its church spire.

It's March 2014 and we've had continuous storms since 29 November. I'm under pressure. I'm trying to produce my first series for RTÉ; it's taken years of work to get to a level where

I can get broadcaster commissions. The BBC called to ask me to film scenes for their *Atlantic* series – such opportunities don't come around too often in a lifetime.

I've spent a lot of time at sea around the Cliffs of Moher in the last ten years, lots of days filming big seas and 'the wave', an ocean monster that rises at an area of cliff known as Aill na Searrach. I never sleep much the night before, so many things to worry about with the boat. All the days out there, bewildered by the mesmeric, elemental beauty of the wave and the cliffs. I say mesmerising, because it dazzles your senses, rising like an all-conquering beast before you; how can this be happening right in front of me? The sound, oh the sound, that crack when the lip of the wave slaps down on itself, the clarity of the echo bouncing off the 700ft cliffs and the conjuring up of a 20ft barrel, surfer nirvana, a tunnel beneath a hundred tonnes of sea water that exists for perhaps three seconds and then disappears, the myriad shades of turquoise, blue and white.

I'd spent years watching the wave and thinking about how I could document it from the sea, in all its uniqueness and angry beauty. I'd managed to get a camera and set of lenses that could accomplish that now, but in a full year, I'd only managed to get to the cliffs once.

Photographer George Karbus was mad to shoot the wave from sea level, and Rob, a local surfer who I knew a bit, came to drive the RIB while we shoot. We knew the wind was going to rise up to 60 knots, but all the charts showed it holding off until six o'clock, low tide was at 1.30, just when the wave breaks at its beautiful best, I convinced myself we'd get out there in our five-metre RIB, have a couple of hours filming and be back before it hit.

On the way out, we held off for a while to watch Cill Stiffian break, there's a gully maybe a few hundred metres wide on the north side where it doesn't break and you can pass through safely, but reading where that is can be tough. Too far south and a big set of waves could catch you, too far north and sets rise suddenly on the shallow ledge and you're on top of Ceann Cragga – Rocky Head; could it be any more obvious, but that's Irish place names for you, they simply tell you what's there.

We took a run at the gully, my stomach in knots, and at some point I realised we'd be OK. The first time you pass out of the bay on a big day and meet the monstrous rolling swell of the open ocean, it's terrifying – at least when you've done it a few times you know what to expect, but your senses never stop telling you the 15ft high rolling swell might just break before you.

We round the cliffs towards Hag's Head and no matter how scared I am, I never cease to be awestruck by the ancient rugged beauty of the Cliffs of Moher from the sea. Swirling fulmars only give a sense of scale, and you embrace vertigo looking up at them. It took me a while to realise that the giant holes that open up 15ft deep in front of the travelling boat are caused by backwash as the swell hits the cliffs, rebounds and smashes into its sister swell; you think the RIB will fall down into them, and I've no

FOLLOWING SPREAD: *Californian big-wave surf legend Rusty Long charging at the Cliffs.* PHOTO: GEORGE KARBUS

doubt some can do damage, it's what seamen wonderfully call 'confused water'.

By now I know things aren't right. From three miles away I can see the wave isn't breaking like it should. It needs offshore or light winds, but the wind has already turned onshore and is beginning to feel threatening.

~~~~~~

I always feel somewhat ancillary to the situation when the wave is being surfed. My exploits are insignificant compared to these men and women. Filming the action from a boat, I'm mostly safe and mostly dry, whereas the surfers are shivering in 9 or 10 degree water, mostly unsure what the next wave will bring and the ever-present option of a serious thrashing and 'hold-down' under a hundred tonnes of water and possibly a long swim to the base, before a long cliff climb to land. The wave was first surfed in 2006 and ever since has drawn big-wave surfers from all across the globe, hardy ocean chargers willing to brave the biggest and best of winter swells for a few moments of ecstasy. The commitment of some of these guys is staggering, with months, sometimes years of preparation. In the early days they used jet skis to get a tow into the ideal position to surf across the face of the wave. Then, after a few years, paddling into position came to be seen a purer form of surfing, but that's multiple times more difficult and requires extraordinary levels of athleticism. The wave breaks here because ocean swell that may have travelled thousands of kilometres, all the time building in size, smashes into a reef where the water depth changes from forty metres to perhaps four in just a hundred metres' distance. The consequence of this can be lumps of water with faces 50 feet high, which I've seen. Terrifying natural beauty. I had actually been hoping to film empty waves without surfers, but that can be a tough ask when the wave is pumping!

~~~~~~

I realise long before we get to Aill na Searrach that it's futile, but maybe in a self-serving exercise or maybe for the sake of the two boys with me to show them there's no point, we continue. When we arrive, I waste no more time and say we're going to have to run for home. No one argues.

I can't recall much about the way back to Cill Stiffian other than anxiety. Sitting in the 15–20 ft swells outside the reef, the wind is now a monstrous 60 knots, 110 km per hour, Beaufort scale 11, violent storm force. The big sets are breaking all the way across the gully. We could drive to the south end of the bay, but we don't know that area in these conditions, and at least we know what happens here. It's simple in one sense: we have to time our passage between big sets, I know from experience we can't outrun the waves, even at full throttle they pass us out and that's without them breaking, I figure when a wave breaks over, the peak and resultant white water will travel even faster.

I brought surf photographer Mickey Smith, a pioneer of big-wave exploration in Ireland, here one February on our way back from the cliffs to watch Cill Stiffian break. The moisture-laden light of the winter sunset behind Cill Stiffian lit the place like a post-nuclear scene. When the wave broke it was like Teahupoo, the infamous Tahitian wave, but in freezing North Atlantic conditions. 'Teahupoo on LSD,' someone commented, a scary acid trip, a barrel big enough almost for our RIB to stand upright in and the fattest shoulder I've ever seen on any wave.

I asked Mickey if he thought it could be surfed. 'I'll get the boys out here,' he replied quietly. He did, and big-wave surfer Fergal Smith told me, 'Never again.' Cill Stiffian was the worst wipeout of his life: the boulder reef pushes the wave up on a grand scale, but unlike a reef break close to shore, which keeps the pressure on the water, here the reefs fall away and all the wave energy drops back into the deepening water, a sub-aquatic tornado.

All of this sits with ice-like clarity in my mind. I interviewed 93-year-old Tomás Ó'Conghaile from Inis Oírr about *Lá mór on gaoithe Duath*, the day of the great north wind, February 1944. There was so much demand for fish during World War II that many Aran immigrants came home from England to fish. Tomás' currach and four others set out from Inis Oírr before dawn that day to fish ling. When the currachs were full to the gunnels with fish, the wind rose like a great monster from the north, then the tide turned and a battle became a war as wind fought against tide, tearing up the sea. '*Bhí an farraige bhriste ón Oileán na Caorach go Ceann Cailleach*,' he told me. 'The sea was broken from Mutton

Wave breaking at Cill Stiffian reef. PHOTO: AARON PIERCE, LIQUID STORM

Island (off Quilty) to Hag's Head.' Nine miles of white water. They had nowhere to go, Cill Stiffian had closed off Liscannor Bay and they were at their limit just to keep their crafts facing into the wind; side on could have been fatal.

I have no doubt that a currach with its native oarsman was the only boat that could have survived those conditions. They knew things would improve when the tide turned, and they could row for home if they could only last that long. The oddest thing he said to me was they discussed whether throwing the fish overboard would help their plight, making them more buoyant, but they decided the fish, even dead ones, would help their buoyancy. Whether it did or not, they did make it back to shore after six hours rowing into that north wind.

That ability to stay calm stayed in my mind. There was only one way past Cill Stiffian; we had to get a feeling for the sets of waves and judge when to make the call. I felt an enormous responsibility to get these men home. At some point we just had to call it, and mostly on feeling. Gently bring up the throttle to full speed, pick a straight line and, more for my benefit, tell the boys they need to

Cill Stiffian reef on a calmer day. PHOTO: AARON PIERCE, LIQUID STORM

hang on, as if they needed to know. It's still the most scared I've ever been.

Looking back would have been futile. I could have done nothing about a breaking wave behind us, so at full throttle I just stayed as true as I could to my line for Liscannor and drove as fast as our Honda outboard would push us. Then, halfway through the passage, the engine cut out.

A large cork was attached to the ignition key, the kind leisure sailors believe will save their keys if they fall overboard. We were getting so smashed that the weight of the cork had jerked the key out of the ignition, and it took at least 15 seconds to restart the engine. Moments later when it happened again, Rob grabbed it and tore the cork off the keyring, restarting the engine. I admired his clarity of thought but couldn't miss his sense of deep urgency.

And then it happens. I hear a fiendish crack behind and turn around to see a mountain of white water chasing us down. It's funny how you can think so clearly and so quickly when you're in trouble. There are several more reef breaks to swim through in order to reach the nearest land point at a place where we could climb the cliffs, a tiny bay known locally as Hayes' Hole, which featured a wave known as 'Chicken Run' by local surfers. I could have throttled north-east towards there, knowing the white water would catch us, but shortening our subsequent swim to land. Chicken Run is a funny wave that some fellas swear works brilliantly in the right conditions, but today it's like a fire-breathing dragon guarding the treasure-laden cave of our safety at Hayes' Hole.

Just to get back to our families, to see my children.

The water is at its coldest in March, 8 or 9 degrees at the surface, colder below. Getting smashed in the white water of one of those reefs has no equivalent – I can't say it's like this or like that, because in my experience there's nothing similar, except to say that it drains your energy, throws you around like a plastic bag in a tornado, and lets you up only when its random, violent energy has run its course. The notion that you can take a few of those beatings in 9-degree water and then swim a couple of miles home, is, at least for me, fanciful.

We could try to stay together in the water, but how would that help? It would only severely impede individual chances of survival. I didn't know Rob very well, he was a decent surfer and fairly fit looking, but of the three of us probably only George stood a chance of swimming back to shore. He was still a young man and unnaturally strong and fit; good genes combined with lots of swimming around in wintry Irish waves have conditioned him to be one of the few men I know who could survive this. Despite my overwhelming concern for his safety, in the darker side of my mind, I know that in this cauldron there'd likely be nothing any of us could do for each other anyway.

Old fishermen tell you they never learnt to swim because it's easier to drown quickly. I know it would be brutal because I'd never stop trying; in all the things I've tried in my life, many of which I've been mediocre at, my main attribute was just to never give up. I suppose I'm one of life's dogs.

Funny how you can think all that in a few seconds. In my raw instinct for survival I turn to my right and my senses more than my logical mind steer the RIB 45 degrees to the south, exactly in front of the worst area of where Cill Stiffian breaks. I still don't know why I did it other than that it felt right. Much later, looking at the admiralty charts, I see that the same freakish bathymetry that causes the wave to break into deep water also swallows up the surface-wave energy as the water and seabed deepens back down to thirty metres … it will hold an already submerged surfer down, but also allow an inflatable boat to stay afloat, albeit with a rocky ride.

No one says anything. I've lost my hat in the wind, which is now so strong that the raindrops are like sharp pebbles being shot at your face from an air gun, but I'm elated. The two boys slowly thaw out and begin to make some chat, someone says this is pure misery, it's still a half-hour drive back to the harbour in these seas, but I turn and say, 'I couldn't care less about that rain, thank sweet fucking Jesus, we'll be home tonight.'

It's still the most scared I've ever been.

LEARNING

For my father

Another January and I'm not at your grave remembering
Not here, in this wet Clare soil.
I see you watching the August tide, saying it won't be long 'til
    the mackerel are in
And warning of fairies in the *paircín*, how horses won't stay
    there after dusk
I see you pulling fishing nets across your seventieth summer
Wrestling with nature to your mutual content
Up the gravelly wet beach at Cuan Éamainn
To the sanctuary of marram grass in fine sand
For cleaning.
And all the other little place names
That kept your ancestors' wonder alive, and lit up how we
    spoke of them
Poll a Phúca, Lán na Choise and the Crow rock.

When we stood watching waves at Béal Gheal,
The sea bearing under a darkened sky,
And you said the word, swell,
I understood of the men and children who had drowned on
    your island.
Passing on to me, the learning.

SHARKS

SHARK. The word conjures up a certain imagery. Its uses within our language are myriad, yet I can't think of one that is complimentary to the animal. As fast as a shark, as sleek and beautiful as a blue shark, as strong as a great white. No, you'll find no such imagery or associations in the modern English language. But basking sharks were revered in ancient Irish culture and I suspect also in those of many other indigenous peoples around the world, who viewed nature very differently. There are legends of Hawaiian shark gods controlling the fish populations.

Like most people, I knew very little about sharks for a lot of my life. I knew of basking sharks from my father, *Liamhán gréine* in Irish meaning sun shark, which made them sound docile. But my father didn't know everything. Sailing from Wales to Ireland many years ago, we spotted creatures rising and blowing in a rolling fashion and I immediately declared my ancestral knowledge of the ocean. 'Basking sharks,' I confidently told my friends, until one of the girls on board mused, 'But they're blowing, doesn't that mean they're mammals?' I took my embarrassment with humility and we collectively agreed they were porpoises, which they may have been, but they could easily also have been common or bottlenose dolphins. In the old days, you see, any animal seen close to shore was either a basking shark or a porpoise.

I first encountered sharks in the water while learning to dive in Byron Bay, Australia, in the 1990s: a pair of wobbegong sharks, docile, bottom-dwelling creatures, who just, well, sat on the seabed all day. Later, diving out on the Great Barrier Reef, a shark approached our boat just as we'd left the water. The dive operator began throwing bits of dead fish overboard and somewhat comically encouraged us to 'Jump in and swim with a shark.' We were confused – was this safe? Based on the notion that a commercial dive operation wouldn't want a dead diver, I got back in with what was some kind of small reef shark. I was surprised at the animal's curiosity, though my trust in the dive operator would prove to be utterly misplaced when, on the next dive, we were dropped in on the shallowest part of the outer reef on a running tide and found ourselves in four or five knots of current, holding on for dear life to lumps of ancient coral and regularly breaking them off. It took the boat 45 minutes to collect us all; my wife Katrina and I were the very last, having drifted nearly 900 metres. It was terrifying. This was a couple of weeks after another local dive boat – with which we also dived – had left two American divers out on the reef. They were never found. So much for human competence.

~~~~~~

Back in Ireland I went on to swim with and film basking sharks many times over the years, but these are docile, non-toothed creatures; the only dangers are that if you get too close and spook them they can take fright and instinctively shudder, which given their size of up to eight metres can be dangerous. They can also breach clear out of the water with the remote possibility of landing on you, and they do weigh 5 tonnes – but mostly, we're the ones disturbing them.

The first time I filmed a basking shark was off Brandon Head, Co. Kerry, in early summer. Sharks have an array of tiny electroreceptors around the front of their heads known as 'ampullae of Lorenzini', which can detect the tiniest of movements, so I had stayed perfectly still in the water, waiting for the animals to approach. They swish their bodies from side to side, propelling themselves with their tail fins, enormous mouths agape to gather zooplankton, which is comprised of tiny fish, shellfish larvae and other microscopic creatures.

This one animal, about eight metres long, approached and I was scared, as no matter what people tell you, these are enormous animals and the sea is not our natural habitat. Seen up close the shark looked truly prehistoric, magnificent, though it was just going about its business feeding. Its skin looked tough and sometimes wrinkled, and reminded me of that of elephants I'd seen in the Serengeti. Gliding right underneath me, the shark touched its tail fin off my belly and immediately shuddered, emptied its bowels and dived to the depths. We never saw it again.

~~~~~~

FOLLOWING SPREAD: Mako shark mid-Atlantic.
PHOTO: GEORGE KARBUS

But toothed sharks were now more interesting to me, blues, por-beagles or perhaps even short-fin makos, all of which are known to visit Irish waters, although the latter two are extremely elusive. In 2013 George Karbus and I decided to try and find blue sharks in Ireland and swim with them. George had photographed them extensively in the Azores, but that was in crystalline water with lots of blue sharks, even makos. We had seen a photo of a blue shark in Ireland, but weren't sure if the photographer had been in the water or just leaned overboard, but to our knowledge no one had been in the water and filmed them.

That was until I went searching film archives and found some fascinating documentaries: one from the 1970s, made at the Cliffs of Moher, featured a South African underwater cameraman being lowered in a cage and shooting a blue shark on a 16mm film camera, brilliant stuff for the time. I found a 1950s tourism film presented by what looked like a near-teenage Terry Wogan promoting shark fishing tourism in Kinsale, Co. Cork, the highlight of which was an Italian man in tinted glasses reeling a blue shark on board, which was immediately battered to death while the angler smiled triumphantly for the camera. 'Yes,' a woman hotelier who seemed to have walked off the set of an Alfred Hitchcock film declared to the camera, 'The fish, you see, people will come here for the fish.'

Sharks have been around for 400 million years, since before dinosaurs even, and have survived mass extinctions of life on earth. That they have remained in more or less the same physical and physiological state for the last 150 million years, is testament to their near-perfect adaptation to the world in which they hunt and survive. That is until they encountered *Homo sapiens*.

I have a family heirloom, a diary kept by an aunt, Bridget O'Sullivan – or Sister Melbride as we knew her – who joined an Ursuline Sisters convent in the late 1930s and, along with her younger sister Catherine, was shipped to Australia to join a burgeoning Catholic Church. Melbride wrote daily observational and hugely descriptive notes of her journey by ship on the SS *Mongolia* of the Cunard line to Australia in 1939. She gave her life to the Church and to the people of Brisbane as a schoolteacher and later ran a shelter for 'desperate' women until her death in 2005.

While in port somewhere in the Red Sea, Melbride gives an account of how men from a local island catch sharks for their meat, and to make a soup from the animal's fins, which they believe cures various illnesses. So I guess shark-fin soup has been around for a long time, albeit only in human terms. So too were witches' potions, and the notion that unpalatable animal body parts, eyes, horns and even testicles, could cure human ailments from cancer to impotence to ageing.

Shark-fin soup is referred to as a 'traditional medicine' in China and can cost up to $100 a bowl. It became hugely fashionable for the burgeoning nouveau riche to display wealth at Chinese social gatherings, and weddings in particular, and offering shark fin soup to impress guests and cure all their ailments. The reality is that shark fins are made of cartilage, and are not only tasteless (the soup has to be flavoured with chicken stock) but have no medicinal qualities that any credible scientist has ever described. I understand some progress has been made in recent years by Chinese media and sports stars campaigning against the scourge of killing sharks for an expensive, medically useless, placebo soup. The emperor is truly naked.

By 2013 scientists estimated that somewhere between 70 and 100 million sharks were being slaughtered globally every year, mainly for their fins of which most shark species have eight. As shark fins were multiple times more valuable than their meat and took a fraction of the deck space, fishermen began cutting fins from live sharks and returning the often still-alive animals to the sea where they would slowly drown due to their inability to swim and pass water over their gills to extract oxygen and breathe.

But it's not just the Chinese that are at fault: shark cartilage has been used extensively in 'cartilage pills', a treatment for joint problems and even cancer, mostly for ageing Europeans and Americans, though there would appear to be little or no research proving that it helps.

It's difficult to tell people in developing countries that they shouldn't catch and sell sharks when they live on the threshold of poverty, but many millions of sharks are also caught by longlining trawlers of richer countries, particularly Japan and Spain.

Sharks are apex predators, meaning they are at the top of the ocean food chain, a role which regulates the numbers and feeding habits of all the animals they eat. Scientist's refer to this role as being like a 'keystone', the central stone at the summit of an arch which locks the whole together.

Slaughtering apex predators of an ecosystem therefore, for highly suspect human medicine is not only morally and ethically wrong, it is ecological suicide. Destroy the ecosystems of the oceans, and we ultimately destroy ourselves. Not to mention millions of other species.

~~~~~~~

Of the 400 global species of sharks, about four are known to be aggressive to humans: great whites, oceanic whitetip, tiger sharks and bull sharks, also known as Zambezi sharks, where they enter the river of the same name in Africa. Aggressive is somewhat misleading though. Sharks are apex predators and territorial animals.

Many shark attacks occur at dawn and dusk: I couldn't confirm it scientifically, but in my years of trying to film ocean predators, hunting activity often seems to peak in the low light of these periods – a simple explanation would be that a predator has a greater element of surprise in low light. Surfers seem to be most prone to shark bites, usually leg or arm bites, i.e. those body parts submerged in the surf zone: after that, scuba divers and swimmers.

I'm not sure you could count the numbers of times people get into the oceans annually, be it to surf, swim, dive, snorkel, kayak or any of the myriad other things we now do in the sea. Say we took a guess that 20 per cent of the 8 billion humans enter the sea twice a year – that's conservative, but let's go with that figure of 3.2 billion human sea entries. There are, on average, six or seven annual human fatalities from shark bites: of course, while you have a greater chance of being bitten if you're swimming in the opaque waters of the Zambezi river or surfing in Western Australia than you do if you're scuba diving in Ireland, those odds are about 500 million to 1. I'm not much of a betting man, but I think I'll take my chances.

Why then do we humans inherently fear a shark attack, even in countries like Ireland and the UK where I can find no credible record of a shark attacking a human in the sea? We have a primal fear – in what we perceive to be a threatening situation such as, say, swimming in the sea – of not being able to see what's below us.

Peter Benchley was a writer who spent a lot of his life in seaside towns along the coasts of Long Island, New York and Cape Cod. He wrote the book and screenplay for Steven Spielberg's 1975 blockbuster *Jaws*, a terrifying, thrilling piece of cinema, even today. I've read a lot about the making of *Jaws*, which went way over time and budget and apparently pushed the young Spielberg to his limit. They'd built a robotic shark, which was to rise from the sea and terrify viewers, but at some point Spielberg and his team realised 'it just wasn't working' and, mid-production, decided to adapt to a Hitchcock style of implied fear and suspense. Watching the movie, the tensest moments aren't when you see the overgrown great white shark, but when its presence is implied, usually in the vicinity of the juxtaposed subject of an innocent child or mother – in fact as I recall, we don't actually see the shark for the first hour of the movie.

James Joyce said that all good writing is about suggestion, and by implication bad writing relies on statement. Good film-makers, novelists, artists and especially poets try to stimulate our thoughts so that we imagine their scenes; our minds have much greater powers of visualisation, which has a far greater impact than any artist or writer can describe. My friend, veteran broadcaster Pat Butler, always said that 'the best pictures are on radio'.

When *Jaws* was on general release some journalist wrote, probably in awe and admiration, that millions of people will never 'get in the sea again'. He was correct.

Some years after *Jaws*, Peter Benchley was scuba diving in the Bahamas when he felt a presence behind him and turned only to realise he was face-to-face with a great white shark. Afterwards, with great honesty, he reported that his first thought had been that, had this animal killed him, it would have been natural justice.

I think not of the millions of people who stayed away from the sea, but of the many millions of sharks likely slaughtered on the basis of fear and prejudice from the impact of *Jaws* on our perception of sharks. But I don't blame Benchley or Spielberg. *Jaws* was and is an incredible movie; it just shouldn't have been the sole basis of our education and understanding of sharks.

Benchley's great white observed him curiously for a few moments before gently swimming away, leaving him a changed man. He dedicated much of the rest of his life to shark conservation, creating awareness of the true nature of these magnificent creatures.

~~~~~~~~

In the summer of 2013 we chartered an angling boat in Clare and the skipper took us to a 'mark', a known catch spot, about ten miles west of Loop Head. We spent a couple of days 'chumming' the water. Chum is a mix of fish, usually mackerel minced up with fish oil and bran – you fill an onion bag, hang it off the boat and wait. The bran keeps the concoction afloat and the oil carries the scent of fish with the tidal current; you can see the oily slick spreading from the boat. Sharks have a powerful sense of smell, though not nearly to the levels in some sensationalised documentaries.

We had a couple of small blue sharks approach the boat and one larger animal on the second day, but it was so difficult getting close to them. There was some swell running, and when you're at the sea surface bobbing up and down while looking at a camera screen, it can get nauseating. I'd made the unwise decision of eating a large salad, the dressing of which had liquefied with some mayonnaise during our rocky 10-mile boat journey. Not long after getting back into the water, I threw up the lot – the skipper was shouting at me to get back on board, but the boat was not designed for swimmers and we had to haul the 21kg camera housing up the high sides with a rope, then remove my long freedive fins before climbing up a ladder at the back. 'I'm all right, I'm all right, gimme back the camera, I'm staying here,' I retorted. I wondered perversely if my lunch might help draw in some sharks, but we left without any useful footage.

I talked to a lot of experts around the country about where to look for sharks and Dr Edward Farrell, a brilliant young shark scientist with whom I'd previously worked, suggested we try Mark

Gannon at Courtmacsherry Sea Angling, a vastly experienced charter angling operator. Mark was a gentleman, with a lifelong knowledge in finding sharks off the Cork coast.

George and I arrived at his B&B in West Cork the night before we were due to go to sea. Mark cleared his throat more than once and asked again: 'Are ye sure about swimming with the sharks?' A group of German anglers who'd spent a week fishing with Mark, were on their celebratory last night. One asked nervously: 'You really gonna swim with sharks?' 'We hope so,' I answered. They erupted into group laughter. 'I wish I could stay to watch you,' quipped another.

Mark took us twenty miles offshore, we caught lots of mackerel and chummed and waited, and waited some more. After perhaps a couple of hours, a small blue shark appears: I slip into the water but the animal darts away immediately. We try many times and with different tactics to get the sharks to stay around the boat, until eventually two or three largish blues swim inquisitively towards me. With great relief, I press the record button, but am instantly distracted by a booming noise. I look up to see the surreal scene of a military helicopter maybe a hundred feet above me, so close I can see the guys in combat garb looking down at me, frowning in fact. What the fuck is this? Mark comes over the side of the boat and shouts down, 'Ken we have to go, there's a navy munitions exercise and we're inside their ten-mile limit, we have to move!' I shout back, 'Ah Jesus Mark, tell 'em we've been at this for days, tell 'em it's for telly, tell 'em anything, please!' Mark gets back on the radio and argues we were more than ten miles from the ship, but I guess it's always futile to argue with an army. 'Ken, the pilot says we have to move – that's it.' Then with a bit of a grin he adds: 'He also said, will you tell that guy in the water there are two sharks circling him.'

Sometimes you have to laugh.

We move, and spend another few hours on a mark over a sunken trawler in about 90 metres of water. Blue sharks eventually show up, first just a few smaller ones, and then up to twelve or thirteen, seeming ever larger. Angling skippers pride themselves on estimating fish sizes, and Mark feels the bigger animals are 2.7 metres long. It's my first time in the water this far offshore, and looking into the sun – what photographers call backlit – the water is green with golden rays of sunlight shooting down into the water: in Irish we call them *Cosa na gréine*, the legs of the sun. With the sun behind, the water looked blueish, almost tropical, we are on the edge of where run-off from land affects the sea water, the open ocean is blue and clear, coastal waters are green and more opaque. There's an old whaling song, 'Sailing from the blue to the green' – green water heralded home for these hardy crews who often spent years at a time at sea.

George Karbus is a truly amazing photographer; you have to see his work to appreciate how beautiful it is. Like myself he wasn't always a lens man: he took up photography after his arrival in Ireland from the Czech Republic, and becoming inspired by the landscape and particularly the underwater world. George is a freediver: he holds his breath while diving underwater rather than using scuba equipment with air tanks, so as to be mobile enough to get in the best position to photograph the moving animals.

I filmed George freediving with the blue sharks, again and again. It was a feast of nature, the sharks stayed with us for the three or four hours we were in the water. We probably did forty or fifty free dives and in my last couple of dives things started to go a little 'black' as my body said enough. Blackout is a serious risk for freedivers and at the end Mark almost had to lift us out of the water. We came back the following day and had it all over again, they circled us for hours, diving and rising, biting the metal boat hull, pushing their snouted heads that resemble Teddy-boy hairstyles into the glass port of the camera housing. Blue sharks are graceful, beautiful creatures, they glide across the water, their streamlined bodies perfected through millions of years of evolution, albeit a process that finished a very long time ago.

Once there were lots of sharks around us, perhaps more than a dozen, they began to behave a bit aggressively, the smaller ones more so, and at some point, one animal smashed into the back of my thigh. I waved to George to come up for a chat. 'They're getting a bit aggressive, what do you think George?', 'Nah, they're fine, they're just playing man,' he answered.

Later that night, over a pint, George cleared his throat. 'Ah Ken, you know when that big blue shark hit your thigh, I must tell you he had his mouth open.'

Thanks, George.

I had looked at their mouths and thought they were too small to get around your leg, but watching them devour a mackerel, I saw that their whole jaws extend, enabling a much larger bite size. A little knowledge and all that ...

George Karbus freediving to a blue shark, twenty miles south of Cork, summer 2013

FOLLOWING SPREAD: *In the water with a blue shark in blueish offshore water.* PHOTO: GEORGE KARBUS

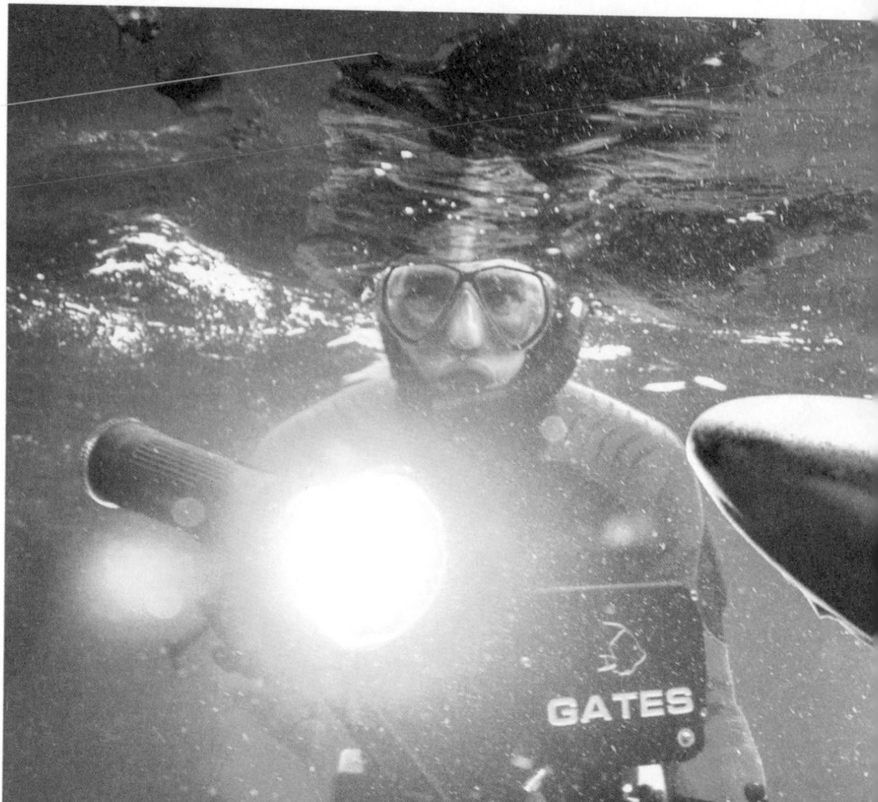
GATES

We made a beautiful scene of these encounters for our RTÉ series *Ireland's Ocean* in 2014, I was very proud to show people in Ireland that there are predatory sharks in our waters, but also to dispel the myth that they are vicious man-eaters. I was especially proud when *The Sun* newspaper devoted a whole page to sharks, and how they're not actually killing machines after all. Every summer, in what journalists call 'the silly season', when there's a lack of news, certain tabloid newspapers run sensational stories about imminent shark attacks, headlines like *Bloodbath on Britain's Beaches This Summer* or *Great White Shark on its Way to Cork*, after a tagged white shark had crossed the mid-Atlantic ridge heading east, but still 1,500 km from Cork. Sadly, some papers reverted to type the following summer, but perhaps we created some awareness of these animals and why we should stop killing millions of them every year.

Inland Fisheries Ireland have been tagging blue sharks since the 1970s in one of the largest shark-tagging programmes in the world, and blues tagged in Ireland have later been seen in the Azores and the US; all of this knowledge has helped to inform us that blue sharks circumnavigate the North Atlantic annually following the seasons and in search of food.

Shark angling tourism is hugely popular in Ireland and indeed globally, presenting coastal communities, many of them traditional fishing communities struggling to survive, with an opportunity for ecotourism and a livelihood. Shark anglers have contributed hugely to research through tagging and logging details of the various species caught, including even porbeagles, short-fin makos and even the enormous six-gill sharks. They have learnt to stop the awful practice of gaff-hooking the animals to drag them on board and most also now use fish bait hooks that are less likely to stay lodged in the animals' mouths and tackle that will degrade in a less harmful way even if it does stay lodged.

However, there is still a custom among recreational shark anglers of lifting up sharks for the trophy photo and keeping them out of the water for too long. Imagine you have no bones in your body, no ribs, just a rubbery spine made from cartilage, so your organs are supported largely by the water. Then after a traumatic half hour of being dragged at the end of a fishing line by a sharp hook lodged in your throat, your full body weight is hauled up onto a boat, an alien environment, and then a few blokes lift you up into their arms, your liver, spleen, intestines are all being crushed by your own unsupported body weight, you're out of the water struggling to breathe and all of this after the chronic stress of what you have perceived as a fight for your life.

I have no doubt that many sharks die after being caught and released. Research has shown some species appear more susceptible than others, but at the very least, anglers and especially charter operators should try to release the animal while it is still in the water and if it must be brought on board to release the hook, the time should be absolutely minimal and the animal handled correctly.

FOLLOWING SPREAD: *A photo that only the likes of George Karbus could capture … a blue shark feeding, with skipper Mark Gannon watching from above water on his angling boat.*
PHOTO: GEORGE KARBUS

I understand the needs of poor people in developing countries catching sharks for much-needed cash so as to feed themselves, even if it is doing enormous damage, but how sad that the human need for the gratification of wanting to impress your mates could actually kill an animal.

As I write, I'm aware of yet another scary shark movie from Hollywood, and newspaper headlines proclaiming *Forty Years of Jawstopia!* Forty years of education, conservation and awareness and millions of people still want to go watch movies about shark monsters.

JELLYFISH AND THE SUN

*All those who adore it shall descend into misery
and punishment.*

ST PATRICK, CONDEMNING SUN WORSHIP

So DIFFERENT. Not actually fish but simplistic creatures lacking a brain, according to scientific notion, which also came to the conclusion that the first life forms on earth were single-celled, jellyfish-like creatures. These were in fact microbes, the fossilised remains of which can still be found in a couple of places around the world within layered rock known as stromatolites. Jellyfish are inherently unsuitable as fossil candidates for obvious reasons, but rare specimens have been dated to 500 million years ago in Utah, China and Brazil.

I've never bothered to articulate why I'm drawn to jellyfish, just that in Ireland we find some of the most beautiful, graceful species. *Nihil est in intellectu quod non prius fuerit in sensu* – There is nothing in the intellect that was not earlier in the senses. That's according to philosophers from Aristotle to John Locke, though others disagree with the notion. I suppose you could say trust your instinct, which is undoubtedly what jellyfish do.

I've spent whole summer days diving in the shallows, filming jellies: moon, compass and the stunning pastel blue jelly. I guess like any cameraman, or perhaps even painter, you document what moves you, rather than what you think should move you.

I recall summer mornings off the Burren shore, hours in the water with just jellyfish for company and celestial sun rays wrapping around and even penetrating the creatures, as I struggled with tanks and lead weights to remain under the animals, keeping them between the sun and my camera. Backlit, photographers call it, but I was feeling rather than thinking. Perhaps it's just my Catholic upbringing that leads me to describe this scene as heavenly.

～～～～～

One of my earliest memories is being on my own in the living room in our house in Ennis, looking out through white net curtains. The room was swamped with golden, celestial light, I faced up to the blinding sun only slightly filtered through the gossamer net. I saw tall figures draped in loose white gowns pass the window, maybe two of them, in along our driveway and under the blackthorn tree that kept guard over our back door. They passed in and out a couple of times, men who I assumed had business with my father.

I wondered who they were. My mother, in the adjoining kitchen, denied any knowledge of the figures. 'The two fellas dressed all in white, they passed the window?' I pleaded. No, nobody there. Well perhaps I daydreamed it, blinded by the sun, or perhaps they were beekeepers come to remove an unwanted nest and my mother wished to keep me away from the situation, beyond that I can find no logical explanation.

But the sun, the sun, it's the source of almost all energy and hence life on our planet, and perhaps others. Scientists may argue about energy sources such as hydrothermal vents, but take away the sun and most all life will eventually die.

No wonder then that we seek it in our lives. It warms and uplifts our consciousness in spring and summer and I love to face into the low sun we get in wintertime Ireland, blinding it may be, but to close your eyes and have it fall on your face is inspiring, almost spiritual for me. I spent some time in northern Norway in November when the sun was setting at 1.30 pm. During the short few hours of daylight, the low sun richly painted the ocean, snowy mountains and rugged landscape. But there was a sense of foreboding in the realisation that darkness was ultimately taking over your existence here. By 4 pm I felt as though it were 10 pm at home and by the third week in November there was no direct sunlight and the sun would not appear again until mid-January. I awoke during the night almost in a panic, the sun, oh my God, how could we survive without it. On my return to Ireland I vowed to never again complain about a dull day.

Scripture speaks about finding the light and it's no coincidence that the word 'celestial' can be taken to mean 'divinity' or 'of or relating to the sun, moon and stars'. Medieval and especially Renaissance religious paintings have a recurring theme of celestial skies, often with shafts of light, theatrically shooting down through

FOLLOWING SPREAD: *Compass jellyfish in vibrant summer colours*

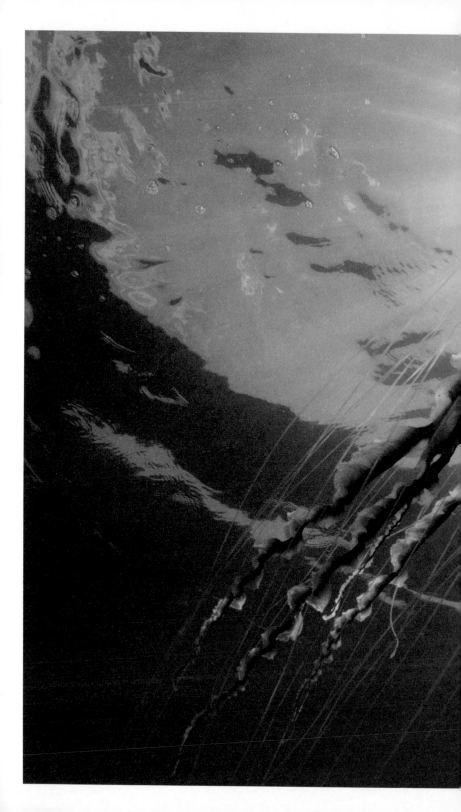

STORIES FROM THE DEEP

clouds to earth, as if they represent a form of divinity inspiring the painting's human subjects. Many if not most of these were painted by artists under the patronage of religious groups.

When I lived in the Netherlands I visited Amsterdam's Rijksmuseum as often as I could, I was enchanted by Caravaggio and Rembrandt. Chiaroscuro is the Italian name for the treatment of light and shade in painting and drawing, and this was central to Caravaggio's work, both natural and candlelit. Many great cinematographers take inspiration from Caravaggio; in fact the aesthetics of much of the ubiquitous medieval drama in film and TV is based around the notion of chiaroscuro and firmly references his work.

I'm not sure I looked at Caravaggio's painting and thought, Oh let's copy that: nature photography is very different to film drama, but I guess like many others, I was influenced by the same elemental light casting across the ocean and earth, enriching textures, colours and even through shadow, the perspectives of the places and creatures upon which it lays its magic.

I walk on Banna strand Co. Kerry in November, and light that has travelled 90 million miles is painting our skies, permeating the moisture-laden banks that are our Atlantic clouds, hundreds of feet thick, some opaque, some with holes giving passage to shafts of light, *Cosa an Gréine* in the Irish language, 'legs of the sun'. Celestially so. Wild patterns changing by the minute, navies, greys and gold, illuminating distant valleys of the Brandon mountains, lighting up wet sand and sparkling specks of silica.

124

Oh the sun, the sun. An enlightened friend told me that the great British sea and landscape painter J.M.W. Turner's dying words were 'The Sun is God.'

~~~~~~

In June and July I often encounter enormous aggregations of moon jellyfish, sometimes thousands of them pulsating together. They've survived the winter as polyps stuck to the seabed, the sun's spring energy then brings life to the ocean shallows, plankton blooms, and, followed by whole ecosystems, these jellies prosper and then peak by midsummer. Among the enormous groups I can see males with their gonads orange and full of sperm and also the clearer-bodied females. The harsh winter, the growth of spring through several life stages and forms, larvae, polyps, medusae and ultimately the maturation into fertile adults of summer, everything has been for this, the chance to reproduce. Many will die along the way in unpredictable ocean currents or poor summer weather, but the thousands that have made it to breed will ensure that the species lives on. Not long after the release of their fertilised eggs the adults die away, leaving their young to overwinter on the seabed as polyps and so the story carries on as it has done for millennia.

In mid to late summer, Compass jellies enrich the shallow waters close to our shores. I dive beneath them to place the sun behind their bodies, as their one-metre legs and stinging tentacles elegantly trail their bell and pulsate them in a particular direction.

Sometimes you'll see tiny fish feeding on scraps of whatever the jellyfish has trapped, seemingly immune to their stings. At a certain point in the summer when they are primed to breed, their colours are vibrant and their bodies strong and intact before they then literally fall apart, and by September I've seen compass jellies minus their legs and tentacles, lying lifeless on the seabed, telling me winter is on the way.

But perhaps the most interesting of all is the Portuguese man o' war jellyfish, seen only recently for the first time in Irish coastal waters. From above the water we see a gas-filled, gelatinous chamber often with luminous pink edges, while underwater its tentacles range from a rich deep purple to a blue akin to a soft children's toy. I filmed one for the first time in Irish offshore waters, along the edge of the continental shelf at the top of the Rockall Basin, 65 km west of Mayo. They are strikingly beautiful; the tentacles seem to flash in pulses as they catch sunlight wavering through the motion of swell on the water surface.

Portuguese man o' war are a collection of different animals working together, but make no mistake, their beauty masks a toxic sting: I've seen hard men almost cry with the pain, which stays for hours or even days, a swimmer friend who was stung told me he didn't sleep for a whole night afterwards.

One of nature's great contradictions.

~~~~~~~

OPPOSITE: *Portuguese man o' war in the blue waters of the deep ocean above the Rockall Basin*

Pelagia noctiluca *jellyfish in warm winter light*

One November day I'd been filming bluefin tuna underwater about fifteen kilometres west of Clare – just Steve Thomas, a vastly experienced sea man driving the RIB and myself, it was a truly amazing day. Smashing into shoals of horse mackerel, tuna are the creatures I'm most afraid of in the water, they move so fast, these large, muscular creatures, and I just didn't know anything about their behaviour and what to expect. I'd been distractedly chasing them for a couple of hours and now it wasn't long to sunset. In the low winter sun I was struggling to find the boat, I'd trust Steve with my life, more than anyone else at sea, but I had to give him a fair chance of finding me – not easy to see just a head bobbing up and down in a winter sea, especially with a black neoprene hood. I was desperately worried at the thought of a fifteen-kilometre swim home, could I even make that? I'd have to ditch the camera housing and even with swim fins and a snorkel, I doubted I could make it that far. And then there's always the risk of a panic, the dread of anyone who spends time in the water … and anyone can have a panic, I've known some of the bravest, most athletic and experienced surf cameramen to lose it in the sea. It's never one thing, but when a few things go wrong as they invariably will, that's the moment you need to find something in yourself, a distraction, perhaps the thought of a loved one, anything to stop the fight or flight response that leads to a panic.

For the umpteenth time that day, the tuna turn and speed off towards another rapidly moving shoal of fish. By now I'm pretty exhausted. As if I need an excuse, I spot a shoal of *Pelagia noctiluca* jellyfish, dozens and dozens of them, gracefully pulsing towards the low winter sun. The sunlight is fracturing into shafts through the uneven sea surface, shooting down in dancing little groups of light, obeying only the movement of the swell. Freediving a few metres below, I look up at this scene, just like the celestial religious paintings of old, except this is very much alive. The *noctiluca* push their bells down around their bodies as a means of propulsion, then retract and push them again as if straining to reach the sun. I hold my camera to the side of one anticipating it would swim across and to my delight it graces the frame, sunlight piercing its now translucent body. Heavenly.

All of the animals' astonishing detail is revealed through the light, the pastel-coloured mottled patterns on its bell and the dozens of tentacles lazily trailing behind, looking innocuous but laden with stinging cells known as nematocysts, which fire on touch.

I relax and take some time to look around, then, rising in the swell, I spot the RIB and a smiling Steve. 'I knew you dived in the sun, and I just kept watching that line.'

SHOOTING
STORMS

IT WAS THE STORMIEST WINTER in Ireland since 1847 according to a meteorologist I met afterwards, though he tends to spend his time in universities.

In early February 2014 Andrew Murray, a BBC producer, called me from Norway and asked whether I could shoot the impending North Atlantic storm about to smash into Ireland for his upcoming documentary series *Atlantic: The Wildest Ocean on Earth*, I was amazed to hear it was flat calm in Arctic Norway. I thanked Andrew and told him I'd been doing nothing else these past months and would be shooting anyway.

This would be the seventh full-category storm we'd had since the end of November. Just after Christmas, two had done severe damage in Lahinch and other coastal towns, and taken a staggering four metres of land away from some of my favourite walking spots on the Clare coast.

But I love storms, when you're able to manage them of course. I've spent years filming them, always trying to capture that special moment, not just the biggest wave, or loudest wind, but something that describes the essence of what's occurring, in a way that a poet might pick a little detail that 'suggests' something greater.

Storms can drain your energy and I'm not sure why. Carrying heavy camera gear, a selection of lenses, batteries and a thirty-year-old film tripod built for stability up and down rocky banks and small cliffs isn't easy, but I've done a lot of that. No, just standing in the midst of 100 km/h winds beside a roaring ocean can make you feel somewhat drained, though it's funny because, in these wildest of scenes, I've found some of my most peaceful moments.

The combination of ten-metre ocean swells with 100 km/h winds and the biggest of wintertime spring tides does the damage. The lunar cycle for some reason dictates that the really big spring tides occur at 6am and 6pm, so winter shooting at the peak of high tides will always be in the dark.

This was day fifteen of trying to document these monster swells, I'd seen plenty of drama but just not captured the scene in a way that I felt described what was happening. Getting enough natural light to shoot and bring some contrast into a scene was proving very difficult. On one day I spent all the daylight hours of 9 to 4.30 pm on the Burren coast, and in all that time there were literally 45 seconds of sunlight, during which time there were no sets of waves.

I think it was some or other sportsman that said the harder I work the luckier I get. Sometime in February and for the umpteenth day, I wandered up along the Burren coast, searching spots I knew, but these were dramatically different conditions from any of the previous storms; this one was a monster. It felt like a lunar landscape, post-nuclear – that term popular in the 1980s, which I guess means desolation, when we were all terrified of a nuclear war.

I found a sheer cliff about 120 feet high; the big sets of waves were smashing up and over the top. Walking in that wind with all the gear was close to my limit but keeping a camera steady, even for slow-motion shooting, was impossible. I tucked my gear behind a large boulder on the lee side of the wind and went searching for some shelter. I found a spot, a ledge really, on the north side of the cliff, slightly lower down and partially sheltered, but with a tricky walk down a slope with some tufts of grass that might give a little grip but was mostly gravel.

I hauled the gear and tried to pace myself, but had one of those moments where you think about your family, your wife and children at home, waiting. Falling here would be an instant fate, though not an instant death … there'd likely be some time being smashed around in that swell, like a rag doll in a liquid tornado that meets a rock mountain.

But I managed to settle onto a tiny grassy verge, got the tripod set, used some rocks to bolster it until it seemed reasonably steady, though the big gusts still made it jump, even when I leaned with all my weight to keep it down.

It was close to sunset when some grudging light appeared on the horizon below the clouds. I started to roll the camera on these gargantuan waves smashing into the Burren cliff – wow, this is going to be incredible. Then from nowhere a guy walked into the shot at the top of the cliff; he must have seen my car back on the road. I screamed at him, but that was futile; I thought about climbing back up and asking him to move but I couldn't trust that my gear wouldn't blow over. I was fit to cry in helpless frustration

Storm on the Burren coast 2014

when I looked again through the viewfinder, I thought, you know what, this mightn't be bad, this gives the shot scale and tells a story. A couple of the guy's friends arrived, I can see a girl shouting at him from a distance, but this motivates him to step closer to the cliff edge. And then it came. A true monster.

I find it amazing that many of these waves originate in Caribbean storms, some 3,000 miles to the west. They roll across the ocean surface, joining together in angry chatter and sputter, mutating into bigger, gnarlier sets of waves, maybe three or four days in passage across the Atlantic, with a gift for us.

And this one was a mutant mass of water, cast from the ocean by an angry, desperate master, sent to test the authenticity of 300 million-year-old stone. Up, up it goes along the cliff face, explosion after explosion bouncing back off stone, seeming to grow stronger rather than weaker as it should have. My friend sees it a little too late, and though he slips a foot in survival response, he scampers back for safe ground as the spray spits at him like a fire-breathing dragon, almost ceremonially displaying its unconquerable power. But nothing defies gravity, though even as it dissipates back down the cliff, small explosions spit vitriol, like an ageing punk rocker at taunting teenagers.

Funny how you can think so much in a moment. Or perhaps it's that our thoughts occur at light speed compared to the limitation of language in describing them.

That was about 4.30 pm in the very last of the light. I packed away the gear, sat on the tiny grass patch, and in the darkness of the full tide at 6pm, I watched alone even bigger, angrier waves dwarf the cliff and smother where the guy had been standing.

~~~~~~

In early December 2014 another North Atlantic deep low-pressure system was about to hit Ireland and Scotland. I was poring over weather charts and talking to locals up and down the coast, but it was hard to know where best to be. I decided to drive south to Cork, where the most concentrated isobars were heading, but an hour down the road a chart update told me the storm was taking a shimmy northwards, so I turned for Donegal, just a six-hour drive on our coast roads.

On the way I stopped to watch Mullaghmore in Sligo, a monster wave that's home to the bravest of surfers on 40-foot days, but not today; it was out of control. Lots of people had come out to watch.

I was worried about my car on this massively exposed coast, it was dancing in the gusts like a fat walrus waddling down a beach, its movements looking distinctly uncomfortable. Others didn't seem to mind, but I moved on.

Lots of stops later I got chatting to an RNLI man in Bundoran, Co. Donegal: their lifeboat station was up a slight hill adjacent to a breakwater pier to the west of the town. He smiled and said come back at 6 am for the high tide and you'll see some waves coming over that pier.

Not many folks staying in a Bundoran hotel in early December; this one had met and embraced many a great storm and bore scars of leaky, loose windows. The gales hollered through empty corridors and whistled under bedroom doors; it was one of those nights when it would have seemed natural to fall in love with a stranger, sheltering together. I sleep only in spells, and in my dreams I somehow explain the intermittent banging outside my door, but sometime during the night I go out into the hall to find the door of a fire-hose shaft has swung open and gusts are breathing life into it. I find the latch and close it.

The lifeboat man's word was good. At 5.30 am the pier is an apocalyptic scene. The sea is furious about something. A few brave RNLI men have come to 'mind' their station and in soft Donegal accents, they tell me that last storm broke their main door when a wave poured up the slipway, seeped under the door, and, as the water gathered inside, its collective weight had forced the door off its mounts as gravity sucked it back down the hill. Today they have the doors open ... I wonder about this.

We chat pleasantly for a while as I explain my presence. 'Oh BBC is it, when will it be on?'

The only light is a single lamp post on the pier, though there is a 'winking willy' navigation light approximately thirty metres or so off the end of the pier being submerged every fifteen seconds or so: surfers look for this kind of wave period because it means the swell has travelled great distances to get here and smaller waves have concatenated into much bigger ones. I admired whoever made that light, it seems unaware of its predicament – I film it as one of those poetic moments, illustrating something much greater in a gentle way.

A few of the waves break over the pier, or maybe just the spray, it's impossible to say which is wave and which is spray, but you know, who cares.

Then, at a few minutes past six, almost on cue, a body of seawater comes over the pier like nothing previous to it, but even that is nothing to the next one.

It's like the Hoover Dam bursting its giant concrete face when this angry, ill-formed, monstrous wave smashes into and over the pier: even from their safe distance the RNLI guys make a run for it; one slips and falls, a colleague leans back and drags him up in an instant, the moment frozen in time like one of those iconic images in an American war sculpture. The wave seems to go on forever, a terrifying, angry power from the ocean, making a mockery of the 'breakwater' pier. On and on it goes, almost submerging the 20-foot-high lamp. After the initial explosions it flows like dirty cream, all the time seeming to rise higher over the pier wall, itself perhaps ten feet high. Skins of sea froth decorate its surface as it slithers past, a giant serpent on its way to fulfil some awful deed.

And then all is quiet. Ghostly quiet. One of those rare moments when, as a cameraman and film-maker, you feel truly satisfied, at peace, even in the midst of all the chaos.

It takes a few minutes for one of the lifeboat men to peer around the corner, still thirty metres or so from the water. I shout over 'Are ye OK?' and it takes a couple of goes for him to see me, he gives a thumbs up, but he is ghostly white.

Sometime later their chief arrives, and I hear them explaining that the something 'was a bit bent, but not bad'. The chief, in a fatherly manner, says, 'Done worry about that, aren't ye all OK.'

Andrew Murray cut the scene into his *Atlantic: The Wildest Ocean on Earth* series as the pinnacle moment in a long and building scene on North Atlantic storms, I was thrilled and emotional to see it, and it juxtaposed against actor Cillian Murphy's soft, dulcet voice.

OPPOSITE: *Monster wave on the breakwater pier at Bundoran, Co. Donegal*

POLL A PHÚCA

How it got its name, is a testament to wonderment
But Poll a Phúca held my boyhood fascination
The fairies' cave, beneath the hill at Barrow
Entry at low tide only, no return guaranteed

In golden light at dawn
Sand glistened with silica as the tide drew back
A gift of magic from the fairies
Sleeping now, to renew their powers

Oh you wouldn't want to go there after dusk, my father told me
Watching safely across a channel of racing tide

Older than my father now, bravened and brazened
I searched for Poll a Phúca.
The new golf course, worried about its underworld,
Stuffed Poll a Phúca with limestone boulders
From far away
Locking in the fairies
The magic ceased,
So middle-aged men
Could get out on weekends

Across the Kerry hills

I hear them crying for Poll a Phúca

Mourning voices

Fairy brethren

Grieving missing magic

Or maybe,

That's just me.

AZORES

THE AZOREANS ARE TRUE SEA PEOPLE. Portuguese by nationality, but really a kind of unique folk on their own. They've survived for 500 years on these tiny North Atlantic islands, 1,600 km from mainland Portugal. And they've survived on what they could harvest from the sea around them, often ingeniously and with irrepressible bravery. I ask our Azorean skipper Michael Costa if there are many fishermen left in the Azores, Michael thinks for a moment and looking at me squarely, says, 'Ken, everyone is a fisherman in the Azores.' Every house has a boat outside and every harbour is filled with boats, from small punts in which local men show their children how and where their grandfathers fished, to mid-sized working boats on which men with faces toughened but liberated by the sea spend their days. That's what boats do for you.

Everything about the Azores is unique. Sited on the junction of three continental plates, its land was violently raised from the seabed by the gargantuan collisions of these continents, battles that have lasted for millions of years, and volcanoes that retched airborne the lava contents of the earth's core and which now plasters the island's surface and seashore as dark rock.

For centuries the Azores have been a haven for seafarers and transatlantic sailors, the sight of land and safe berthage a vision after weeks at sea. And for marine animals, it's no different –

Faial
Pico

The Azores islands, 1,200 km west of Portugal and 2,000 km south-west of Ireland. GRAPHIC: PHIL RAFFERTY

oceanic currents and tides drive nutrient-rich water up the flanks of these great volcanoes, creating a mid-ocean oasis. I would guess that large whales have been stopping off here for millions of years on their migrations between the tropics and northern latitudes where many spend the summer months feeding. Humpback whales, sei whales, Minkes, fins, even the almost-extinct North Atlantic right whale have all been seen here, but the holy grail is, of course, the blue whale.

I believe that from seabed to summit Mount Pico is, at 3,500 metres, the tallest mountain in Europe, but there are many mountains in the Azores and most of these mountains are underwater. A feature such as this, rising up out of the seabed, will attract organic matter brought on by tidal currents and upwellings. These seamounts generate consequent growth of algae, which fauna feed on, then fish feed on fauna and so on up the food chain. Blue sharks and huge mobula rays congregate over these seamounts around the Azores archipelago, though some are quite far offshore.

I first went to the Azores, to the island of Pico, with George Karbus, in my humble opinion one of our greatest nature photographers. George had been going there since before it became a popular destination for divers and whale watchers.

~~~~~~~

My first experience of diving into the crystal-clear, azure water was somewhere between trippy and terrifying. With 30-metre visibility and at 2,000 metres deep it's like a form of sensory deprivation; blue is all you can see, there are no objects with which to orientate yourself, you feel no sense of dimension, like a whiteout I once experienced when caught in a snow blizzard snowboarding on an Austrian mountain, terrifying.

We chase, lungs bursting, after enormous bait balls of scad mackerel being hunted by common and Atlantic spotted dolphins, the fish clustering together in the hope of safety or perhaps to appear as a large creature, but dolphins figured that move out long ago, they drive at the shoal from below, pushing them up to the surface where's there's no escape. And from above, shearwaters have also learnt to anticipate this reaction and dive at just the right time by the dozen into the handsomely presented shoal of fatty fish. Underwater shearwaters are graceful, mobile swimmers and maximise their water time to hunt and gather. Dolphins appear to me to be true multitaskers here; in one movement they go from herding and swallowing the fish to sweeping around under the bow of our RIB and breaching the surface – I saw two females suckling their calves while swimming with the pod, a magical, maternal sight to behold.

With all the predators here now the shoal splits into smaller units; one swims under George for shelter, which cracks me up, so I make the shark sign to him with my hand and he looks about nervously, though we're not really scared of sharks, we're hugely respectful, but we know they're not interested in us.

And then an enormous but elusive Bryde's whale powers into the middle of the fish, mouth agape; we can barely make out its shape in the distance but its throat pleats have ballooned open like a giant mouth parachute – and you might say all bets are off on the fish surviving this last attack. I suppose the bottom of the food chain is never a great place to be for any creature.

Our skipper Michael Costa, from three generations of an Azorean fishing family, guides us across the open ocean waters from the islands of Pico and Faial where we meet Risso's dolphins, ghostly figures with grey-and-white scarred skin, often in groups of five or ten.

I encountered the heart-wrenching sight of a female Risso's carrying a dead newborn calf in her mouth. This is something that occurs with cetaceans, perhaps a form of grieving, but then humans wouldn't just dump the body of a loved one and walk away, especially not an infant. We're compelled to stay connected with the remains in some way, at least for a while, to observe some form of death ritual and to treat the body with respect. Dolphins move around the ocean constantly and I guess carrying a lost infant may be a similar form of ritual, possibly preferable to just abandoning it immediately after death.

There are almost half a dozen species of dolphins to be encountered around the Azores, common dolphins, Atlantic spotted, bottlenose, striped and Risso's dolphins. That there are so many subspecies is likely evidence of how long dolphins have been around, as groups evolved differently to adapt to different local conditions.

There's a lot of rubbish spoken about dolphin sensitivity and intelligence and playfulness. How does one measure these traits just by the size of an animal's brain? Dolphins, and all cetaceans, are creatures highly adapted to the world in which they live, a world where acoustics are more important than vision, and they are incredibly skilled at surviving here – broadly speaking, as a species they've been doing this for 50 million years.

But dolphins are also highly sociable creatures; they almost always live in groups, hunting together and, apparently, socialising. Common dolphins, for example, seem to jostle with each other at times, and leap out of the water in unison or sequentially in a kind of formation, though whether this is play or just the way athletic hunters who must always remain on the move live their lives isn't really important, and so human-centric interpretations are superfluous.

~~~~~~~

Late one October evening, a few kilometres west of the old whaling town of Lajes do Pico, when the sun was almost at its lowest, we encountered the unmistakable bushy blow of a large sperm whale, and then as if the animal needed scale to illustrate its 10- or 11-metre length, a group of Risso's began swimming alongside and possibly even harassing the animal. I was in the water in a flash, but sperm whales are very wary of humans, quite rightly so and especially around the Azores where they were still hunted by man within the lifetime of many of the whales here. I managed to film a few encounters with this majestic animal, although it was mostly diving after some surface breaths by the time I could get near. I could clearly see its eye moving and taking stock of the odd creature that was me.

Sperm whales hunt in the deep ocean down to depths of more than 3,000 metres for octopus, squid and even the elusive giant squid, monsters of the deep that can grow up to 13 metres in width; older whales carry the scars across their mouths and heads of what must be a monumental battle between two giants of nature. I'm somehow reminded of Muhammad Ali, hovering over the larger, stronger but now prostrate George Foreman … arms raised in victory but already bearing a punch drunkenness that would scar his later life.

Sperm-whale skin is grey and wrinkled like an elephant's, their small pectoral fins can give calves the appearance of Dumbo, but the adult's enormous rectangular heads are the unmistakable, iconic figure of Herman Melville's Moby-Dick. These heads are largely filled with spermaceti, a delicate waxy white substance reduced to oil by boiling, and the origin of the animal's name. The quantity of spermaceti within these creatures, which in large animals can be almost 2,000 litres, almost led to the decimation of their species it was so commercially valued by human industry of the industrial revolution and indeed two world wars. A victim of their own evolutionary success.

Sperm whales' enormous spermaceti-filled skulls are used to generate and re-receive sounds in a technique known as echolocation, whereby they form a visual image of features and objects in search of their prey in the darkness of the deep ocean, similar to sonar technology used by fishermen. By reflecting the sound back and forth several times within their spermaceti and skull, they can generate focused aural clicks of more than 200 decibels in strength, which can also stun their prey; a jet engine, by comparison, may emit up to 170 decibels. Underwater cameramen have spoken of feeling as though their chests were collapsing on experiencing sperm whale clicks – although these were more likely to be the less powerful communication clicks between animals.

In more than 200 years of global whaling, over a million sperm whales were hunted and killed for their spermaceti oil. That evening in Pico as I witnessed the majesty and 'aliveness' of that adult sperm whale glancing back in my direction as it ran away

FOLLOWING SPREAD: *Sperm whale in the Azores*
PHOTO: GEORGE KARBUS

from me to the depths, I resolved to try and document these animals and do something to help with our understanding of them and ultimately to try to help conserve them.

~~~~~~~

Hundreds of years ago Yankee whalers visited the Azores where they found not only a bounty of whales, but skilled, hardworking seamen, many of whom signed on as whalers for voyages that could last more than two years, even across into the Pacific Ocean. Conditions on these whale ships were brutal, life was cheap, but this is what men did to survive in the world. The bloodied scene of butchering a large whale aboard a rocky ship, removing the entrails, carving a skull hole to reach the spermaceti into which cabin boys were sometimes lowered to reach the last of the wax, must have been a truly barbaric scene. I guess you can 'normalise' anything, but somehow the dark side of traditional or subsistence hunting seems more tolerable than that of industrial-scale destruction of whales.

Azoreans settled in the New England whaling towns of Nantucket and New Bedford and many thousands of Azoreans still live there, much like their island neighbours to the south, the Cape Verdeans, also 'drafted' whale men.

Sometime in the middle of the nineteenth century, with a decline in American whaling, Azorean whale men brought their skills home and further developed them for shore-based whaling, building sleek wooden whale boats for a crew of six oarsmen and a

Azorean whalers with a sperm whale. PHOTO: NATIONAL GEOGRAPHIC

Azorean whaler. PHOTO: NATIONAL GEOGRAPHIC

harpooner. Seamanship was a part of these men, as was inordinate bravery, and they began chasing sperm whales with a hand-thrown harpoon, the six oarsmen holding pace with the whale while the harpooner waited for the right moment to strike, to pierce the animal in exactly the right spot to give it a fast death … a large sperm whale could tow a small craft like this for hours and tens of miles out to sea or even easier, smash the boat and men, sending them to a certain death.

Some years ago, in the small town of Calheta De Nesquim in the month of May, I witnessed the wondrous sight of five young Azorean men carrying an ancient whaleboat through antique wooden doors from a small stone building, under the watchful eyes of a septuagenarian father figure. They had, during the previous winter, lovingly tended to this craft built by their grandfathers and their uncles; everything about it looked perfect, the sleek lines of the hull rising curvaceously and perfectly up towards the bow, the functionality of the stowaway rudder and the perfect pastel colours proudly emblematic of their locality.

This was a craft that had seen monstrous battles, a craft on which men, having kissed the foreheads of their wives and children and no doubt uttered some words of love, had fallen, eternalising those same kisses within the psyche of their loved ones. But this was a craft which also delivered a bounty of subsistence for the islanders, a people more ravaged by immigration than us, the Irish, if you can imagine that. I meet an older man near the beautiful church in Calheta, who tells me he's returned after spending much of his life in Canada. When I tell him I admire the community spirit of his people, he turns to face me. 'But there are only old people here now my friend.' It is the sad and tragic affliction of remote communities, never more so than now in the era of urbanisation all across the world.

~~~~~~

At the height of Azores whaling, there were twenty-seven whaling stations, but the Azoreans were unique because even though they hunted whales for industrial uses, they did so in a traditional manner, eschewing the mechanisation of the explosive harpoon and ships used by other whaling nations.

I climb a few hundred metres up a local mountain to meet Antero, a former whaler, who has for the past twenty years now, used his whaling skills to spot whales for ecotourism, whale-watch operators. He refuses to discuss anything until I tell him who my favourite soccer team is, he's never heard of Galway United so we settle on Liverpool, but his chest rises as he says 'Benfica', standing back proudly as if to admire the word; I clap him on the back and in my broken Portuguese and his broken English we talk whale …

'Este Vigia mea' – this is my vigia, a small stone building he built by hand overlooking an ocean expanse. He tells me he has worked with whales since he was twenty-one, and becomes a little sullen before continuing, 'I was always gone to hunt whales … all the islands were, but it was forbidden by the EU in 1984.' He is unrepentant, and it's clear that he would hunt whales again in the morning if allowed to do so.

He spends twelve hours a day watching the ocean through surprisingly small binoculars, guiding the whale-watch boats to the whale blows. He has spotted whales twenty-five miles away, a staggering feat of visual interpretation, and only something a man who has spent his life watching the sea could manage. In the winter, when there are no tourists, he watches just because he wants to, or perhaps needs to, all the time copiously recording his observations in handwritten notes; his notebooks must hold some incredible stories and accounts, I do hope Antero or someone else gets to tells their tales.

But Antero's is an extraordinary story of how life can change – while whaling money sustained these islanders and built, among other things, ornate nineteenth-century churches in every small town, almost motifs of heady times, whale-watching tourism now provides much-needed employment and cash, and clearly on a more sustainable basis. But such existence is rarely easy.

~~~~~~~

I returned to the Azores in 2016, my third visit to the islands, and now in search of blue and sperm whales. I dreamed up the notion of trying to find blue and sperm whales in Irish offshore waters and then trying to do the same in the Azores in the hope of matching individual animals using photographic identification, as these whales have unique pigmentation much like our fingerprints. Bit of a mad idea really, but naivety can be a doorway to enlightenment. There were perhaps just four or five photographs of blue whales in Irish waters, and I could find just one smudgy photo of a sperm whale here, though a German researcher, Lisa Steiner, now a long-time Azores resident, had matched a dead sperm whale from Ireland to Norway. We know that bull sperm whales move up into higher latitudes as they age, and eventually into Norwegian and Arctic waters. Scientists have been able to identify sperm whale clicks along the edge of the continental shelf to the west of Ireland as being mostly from males, which I find incredible.

Huge photo-ID work has been done with sperm whales around the Azores, and mothers and calves are seen regularly in autumn, so my theory, however innocent, is that bull sperm whales that feed to the west of Ireland might go to the Azores in search of breeding females, it being the closest known breeding grounds.

Scientific theory on blue whales is that after wintering somewhere in the tropics they migrate north to Arctic waters for summer feeding. The tropics, or sub-tropics, could literally be anywhere from east of the Caribbean to west of Africa, an area of perhaps 6 or 7 million km^2. But their summer feeding had been well documented. Richard Sears is a whale research scientist who has studied blue whales for thirty years from his base in the Mingan Archipelago near Quebec in Canada. Richard has photographed hundreds of blue whales and made many matches between north and south latitudes, painstaking, dogged research work. To our knowledge, by 2016 there had been just six long-distance matches of blue whales in the North Atlantic and no three-way matches, i.e. where an individual blue whale was photographed three times in different locations. Such long-distance matches would help confirm these animals' migration routes.

And so in that April of 2016 we returned to our good friends Enrico Villa and Michael Costa at Cetacean Watch Azores on Pico island. For the first week it's just myself and James Blake, a man whose life story makes the rest of us feel like your man in the bible who buried his ten talents to keep them perfect.

We're chatting over dinner about men who've tried to row between continents, I'm saying how crazy it is … 'I did that,' James says politely … 'You what?', 'Yeah me and three lads rowed from Australia to New Zealand, just decided to do it, I guess. Fifty-six days at sea.' And over the next three weeks James politely, almost embarrassingly, let slip several more of these startling revelations. His dad was the legendary New Zealand sailor Pete Blake, winner of successive Americas Cup and a Kiwi folk hero. Pete Blake was murdered by Brazilian pirates while doing environmental work in the Amazon in 2001, when James was just fifteen. After about a week, sound recordist John 'Bob' Brennan joined us, a Kilkenny man whose eclectic company has to be experienced to be understood, and kept us laughing whenever spirits ebbed, and most other times as well.

I'm not much of a believer in luck: you work incredibly hard, use your head and follow your heart and good things begin to happen. I'd trained for months at home, cycling up hills holding my breath in torrential rain, trying to get my body to a level where I could potentially freedive with fast-moving whales. Freediving means holding your breath while diving rather using scuba gear and air tanks. Such equipment is too bulky and heavy for the mobility required to quickly enter the water and dive into position to film a passing whale. On a day trying to film whales, I might climb into and out of the RIB maybe forty times and that would be impossible with scuba gear. Bubbles are also a sign of aggression between whales and so pumping out clouds of bubbles in the presence of whales the size of a double-decker bus may not be a great idea.

It is a truly awful experience to need to breathe but be unable to do so. To look up at a distant sea surface from under the water, one can easily panic in such moments. It appears quite the feat then to hold your breath for perhaps two minutes, but like many things, with some training and practice, most reasonably fit people can learn to breath-hold and freedive for at least short periods. We have enormous, unused capacity to remain without fresh oxygen: competitive freedivers can hold their breath for ten minutes, and the world record breath-hold is somewhere above twenty minutes. Everything about freediving is based on slowing your body's functions down – your heart rate, your demand for oxygen and, most crucially, your mind.

Chasing whales, though, before diving is completely different. You're already in oxygen debt, and then you need to dive and breath-hold at a time when your body is screaming for air. My great friend the superb freediver Kate Hamsikova helped me train with intensive anaerobic swimming followed by breath-holding freedives. Kate put me through my paces in Irish winter seas; swim for thirty metres, dive for twenty, do this ten times across the bay, then back again … after twenty minutes I was fit to pass out. Very *good* Ken, now we'll take a break, that was a very good warm up, Kate says, and I nearly died! But it served me well.

After just a few hours of our first day at sea, Antero tells us across a crackly radio that there is a fin whale just to the west. Michael takes us to within a hundred metres; the animal is just 'lolling' at the surface, I've tried many times over ten years to film a fin whale underwater, always unsuccessfully, and I'd only ever seen them travelling at speed.

Animals can sense your energy levels and heart rate, so remaining as calm as I can, I fin the last hundred metres gently through blue water towards this calm giant. I can see its eye watching me, it remains still for a short while, as do I, and although the minute movement of its tail fin is only barely discernible, the creature then begins drifting away from me. I don't give chase, I keep filming as the enormous tail fin, the width of a small-aircraft wing, drifts across my camera frame.

By not harassing the animal, it remains calm enough for me to have two more encounters as Michael skilfully drops me into its path where I remained still, but James Blake's drone shooting reveals the story with greatest clarity, as a 6ft 4 me is dwarfed by this 20m, 60ft giant.

~~~~~~~

Over the coming days we had more and more success documenting whales; a sperm whale calf swam right up to my camera, curiously taking in the odd sight of a wetsuited human. I could see a cookiecutter shark bite on its pectoral fin and a parasitic remora fish suckered onto its underside, both useful observations for research. Sometimes, when spirited people get together, perhaps energy flows or perhaps sea gods just smile on you, for every day in the Azores was amazing.

But the blue whale was the true holy grail. Antero had somewhat dampened my expectation by telling me that this year he had seen them migrating past the Azores much earlier than normal. Sightings were rare, but had begun to rise over the last two to three years. Blue whales feed on krill, tiny prawn-like copepods drifting on oceanic currents. Everything in the ocean is dynamic and krill aggregations could easily move a few hundred kilometres east or west in different years, drawing the blue whales with them, something which would have a dramatic impact on our subsequent sightings.

Nevertheless we remained optimistic and worked hard, and after ten days or so at sea, we heard the magic words across the radio from the Benfica man, '*Baleia azul* Michael, *baleia azul*' – blue whale, blue whale. Like a kestrel tracking its prey, almost without need of thought, Michael had the RIB in parallel to two blue whales, before the rest of us even saw them rise. And then this enormous muscular creature rose from the ocean, its blowhole as wide as my shoulders, emitting a sound that reverberated up through Bob's microphone and into his mind, forcing him to visibly judder. I saw for the first time the mottled pattern from its neck along its back, and of course why we call them 'blue', but most impressive was the muscularity of this giant as its vertebrae rose and bent back down, allowing it to dive again. I can still see it in my mind, so enormous that it appeared to be occurring in slow motion, almost like a giraffe running, only much bigger.

In no time James had managed to shoot beautiful scenes with the two animals emerging from the azure ocean, first one and then another crossing gently into his camera frame … photographic instinct is something you just can't teach, and James had it in bucket loads.

But underwater was where we really wanted to document these animals, to get close enough to give people a true sense of them in the place where they live. Again and again Michael dropped me into the water ahead of them, but they were travelling at a constant five or six miles per hour, and with poor water visibility after some stormy days, I needed to get within a few metres to see and film them with any degree of detail. It was so tough, you drop in from the RIB and kick your fins like hell for maybe 50 metres, pushing the 21kg camera housing in front and try to be in their line and sit still … then paddle back to the boat and lift yourself and the 10kg of lead I wear for rapid freedive descent up a metre and a half into the boat with the lads shouting to hurry on … you would do this maybe forty or fifty times in a day trying to film fast-moving whales.

We tracked the animals for five or six hours and for perhaps thirty miles (50 km); the only time they changed their course was to turn 90 degrees to the north around Faial Island, from where we followed them for another six to eight miles northwards. This,

Freediving to film a passing blue whale: this is the only shot I have which gives a true sense of the scale of the animal.

we believe, was clear migration behaviour, heading north towards Arctic waters and summer feeding.

I eventually got within maybe ten metres of one of the blue whales, but it was diving and I struggled to follow it, then after a long swim when I was already well out of breath, one animal swam maybe eight metres under me, I had to take a second to catch one more breath, which meant I timed my dive just fractionally too late, and the whale was again too far away to capture its detail. After six hours of this, I was exhausted – in the water I was looking up at the RIB, my arms now just jelly, Michael saw the state of me, he and James reached over and pulled me up into the boat. I'd given everything, but still not had the shot we needed. We did shoot loads of video of the animals above water and I got lots of good stills photos, which would be useful for photo identification.

We began the return journey to our home port of Madalena, Pico, somewhat elated, but I knew in my heart I'd missed the key part of any story I could tell about the blue whale. On the way back we encountered two humpback whales, a relatively rare sighting around the Azores. I managed a few more swims having recovered a bit, but couldn't get close to them. On turning into the channel between Pico and Faial, we gasped – it had been a beautiful sunny day, I had a diver's tan, an oval-shaped sunburned face and pure white under the wetsuit hood. But now we saw a true Atlantic squall between us and our port, dark, foreboding cloud, dumping its contents of fingernail-sized hail stones on anything that dared stray into its path. We braced ourselves, Michael told us we could either drive slowly to lessen the impact of the hail, which would take much longer, or drive quickly and suffer more for a shorter time. We asked him to do what he felt was right. It was like someone shooting small stones out of an air gun directly into your face, you simply couldn't keep your eyes open and needed an arm to cover your face.

In a harbourside café, over a cold, crisp Portuguese *cerveja*, we tried to grasp the enormity of the day. It had taken me two years to get to this point, between research, funding applications, more of the same, then fitness training, equipment preparation, getting us all out to the islands and ready – and in reality I knew I'd missed the moment. Albeit the poor water visibility wasn't my fault, perhaps younger, fitter men would have managed to get those last two or three metres closer to the whale, but there was no point pondering that. We enjoyed the feeling, went to bed and got up to do it all again.

~~~~~~

And so with just two days left on the islands we hopefully, perhaps somewhat mutedly, went to sea again. A bunch of whale-watching boats were out along with the marine police, who were checking that everyone complied with whale-watching regulations, which they always do in Azores.

After a couple of dull hours, the air lit up as Antero's voice called over our radio, '*Baleia Azul, ele está perto de você!*' He's near you. A single blue whale passed me a few times in the water, still murky by Azores standards, I just couldn't get close enough – not surprising really, that a 27-metre animal who's spent millions of years evolving and adapting to life underwater is able to avoid a human in the open ocean.

I stop in the water, close my eyes in sheer frustration and address the animal in my mind: 'Please, please don't be afraid, I mean you no harm, this is something really good that could help you and your species ...' I ask my own ancestors' spirits to help, I

Free diving to film a blue whale. PHOTO: STEFANO ULIVI

think of how close we were to achieving something great. Pathetic, perhaps; there are people who'd snigger, scientists certainly would.

I then hear Stefano, a wonderful Italian man, cry out from our RIB: 'Over there Ken, he's over there!' I swim in the direction he points to, and with a slow and almost dragon-like gyration of its 90ft body, a blue whale emerges from the depths right beneath me. I dive perhaps eight metres, bringing me within a metre of the creature, my camera rolling.

For the next 27 seconds the body of this blue whale passes before my eyes, letting me see and film all of its gorgeous mottled

Happy days in the Azores with our skipper Michael Costa, Stefano Ulivi and cameraman James Blake, after I'd finally managed to dive with a blue whale. PHOTO: STEFANO ULIVI

pattern, and the word 'Leviathan' comes to mind, a biblical word for ancient sea monsters adopted by whalers. My body screams for air as I waited for it to pass and complete the story that has taken years to tell. I hear Kate softly say, be calm Ken, be calm, and I somehow hold my breath until its tail has crossed out of frame – rising to the surface, things began to go a little black, but I'm OK, and Stefano, Michael, James and Bob cheer me back to the RIB, oxygen-starved, exhausted but elated.

This same blue whale, our research would later show, had been photographed feeding in Iceland six years earlier, just the seventh ever North Atlantic long-distance match of a blue whale, but it gets better, when in literally the last week of production, we discover that it had also been photographed previously near the Azores, making it the first ever three-way match of a blue whale in the north-east Atlantic, and conclusively proving that this animal migrated in spring from the tropics, up the Mid-Atlantic Ridge to Arctic waters.

Despite two years of efforts, we weren't able to encounter a blue whale in Irish offshore waters, an area of just 10,000 km² … but through the incredible efforts of our research partners, Maria Iversen, Marianne Rasmussen and Roland Madsen in Iceland and Denmark, Richard Sears in Canada, Enrico Villa and Lisa Steiner in the Azores, Mick Baines and Maren Reichelt in Ireland and Mauritania, and our own Dr Conor Ryan, we matched a blue whale photographed by Maren on the Porcupine Bank west of Ireland in October to the Azores in spring, meaning this animal almost certainly followed the spring northward migration route and autumnal southward route back to the tropics.

These are vital pieces of a very large jigsaw puzzle, functional parts showing where these endangered animals migrate, and why they need to be protected. The largest animal ever to have lived.

BASKING SHARKS

WHAT AN ODD THING it is to want to swim with a shark. In the sea. Us humans, we're usually close to the surface and looking down, into darkness, considering what lurks below.

All our instinctual fears tell us this might not be good.

But it's an interest I've developed over the years and so I've spent a fair bit of time trying to film sharks in our waters. The reality, I discovered, was somewhat different to what my fear implied. Watching an approaching shark, your mind focuses, a heightened sense of awareness comes over you, but passing through the fight-or-flight response, you go on to observe a marvellous marine creature, hundreds of millions of years old, inquisitive and just doing what it does to survive, searching for food.

But not all shark species are quite so docile as the ones I've encountered in Ireland. I wouldn't wish to meet a bull shark in murky waters, or a great white in dawn surf.

In Ireland I've managed to film basking and blue sharks, as well as the smaller tope shark and various dogfish species, our smallest sharks. I've made various attempts to document makos and angel sharks, always unsuccessfully, and seen flashes of the hugely elusive porbeagle, Ireland's largest predatory shark, slightly smaller than but unnervingly similar in appearance to a great white, but haven't yet managed to get close enough to film a porbeagle.

I used to be scared – and you should be respectfully cautious encountering any shark. The ocean is an alien environment for humans and sharks haven't seen many of us, so they're perhaps not sure how to respond, and so it's important to know how to behave around these animals, to understand their behaviour and, most importantly, to know when to leave them alone.

When I first tried to film basking sharks, it took a while to realise that finning after them whilst pushing a camera is a bit like trying to pedal a penny-farthing bicycle up a steep hill. Like all wild animals, in my experience, if they're moving away from you it's best to let them go.

With a bit of help from my old friend John Boyle, who spent years filming them in Cornwall, and from my own observations, I realised that you need to spend enough time watching their paths as they repeatedly trawl the same area, so as to eventually judge where they'll be, and then sit still on that line.

Basking sharks appear in our inshore waters in spring to feed on zooplankton, a collection of tiny eggs and animals that then feed on phytoplankton which is made up of tiny plants that bloom in the sunlight of longer spring days. So the sharks are chasing 'seams' of zooplankton often running with tidal currents. Their snouts and part of their heads are covered with arrays of sensors known as ampullae of Lorenzini, gel-filled pores that can detect the bioelectric fields which all organisms produce. They can track the movements of zooplankton – even, amazingly – through their nightly migration between deep and surface waters. So if these sharks can detect the movements of 2mm pieces of plankton, a human will need to stay very still in order not to spook them.

In the spring tides of early May 2012 I spent several days filming sharks at the south end of the Cliffs of Moher, near Hag's Head. Some of the biggest tides of the year occur at that point, and because this is during a spring plankton bloom, really special things can happen in coastal waters. On the third day, as the tide was at its peak and flowing fastest around the 'corner' of the cliffs, the surface water was pinkish in colour from the density of plankton, like a kind of pasta soup, big hollow pieces, some maybe 10mm wide; you felt as though you could scoop up a saucepanful and cook them. The basking sharks, preoccupied with this bonanza, seemed to lose all caution in my presence and regularly swam within a metre of my camera.

Then a huge shoal of juvenile mackerel appeared below me in the water, drawn by the same bounty, their rich green and silvery pigmentation pulsing and flashing as maybe ten thousand of them flicked and swam in perfect synchronised formation, like an underwater murmuration of starlings.

After five or so hours, we decided to drive the six miles back to Liscannor to get some sandwiches and boat fuel. On our return, perhaps forty minutes later, the sharks and mackerel were all gone. Vanished. The climactic stage of tide and consequent feeding had passed.

~~~~~~

In 2016 we were in full production for *Ireland's DEEP ATLANTIC*, an ambitious natural history series about my journeys out into the deep, open waters of the North Atlantic in search of whales, sharks and any other creatures. I was hopeful about finding certain whale species, but in terms of sharks it was a real unknown. I know many of the underwater cameramen around Europe, but none had been in these offshore waters to the west of Ireland and out to the edge of the continental shelf. Shark scientists would smile when I'd ask what I might find in offshore waters, blue sharks were obvious but after that, hmm ... No one had spent the time looking for sharks in these areas, I guess there are easier places to find large ocean animals!

I've spent ten years pulling RIBs to remote parts of Ireland, days at a time searching for whales, the Saltee Islands off Wexford, the coastal waters of Waterford, West Cork and the Blasket Islands off West Kerry, but for a few years now, I'd been watching a section of the ocean off Clare, where I live. I've seen signs from shore, flocks of birds diving perhaps 15–25 km out from the shore. While sailing home from a two-week expedition on the open Atlantic on board a research ship, I spotted definite bait-ball activity, west of Mutton Island off Quilty, but after two weeks at sea and with our home port of Galway almost in sight, it would have been somewhat awkward asking the captain and thirty-five other sailors to stop the ship so that I could wait to spot a whale blow. On a sailing trip that summer, I'd seen a single large whale blow in the midst of lots of birds; again we were in a hurry for our port and couldn't stop, but there was clearly a fertile area out there somewhere.

I wasn't aware of anyone else seeing this activity until I met a young marine biology student called John Collins, who, it turned out, had also seen whale blows through a spotting scope west of Clare. John agreed to watch from the shore and we launched our (kind of) brand new RIB from Kilkee in mid-August. John didn't have a car, but would, with incredible enthusiasm, pack up his scope and cycle from one headland to another trying to spot whales.

We went out about fifteen kilometres and then drove transects north, i.e. four kilometres west, then two north, then four east, then north again and so on for about five hours, but apart from a flurry of excitement with a few common dolphins and some storm petrels, there were no animals to be seen.

Just as well we had a good crew who liked being at sea, including Kev Smith, our drone cameraman, and pioneering big-wave surfer Peter Conroy – also a paramedic, which was always reassuring. As is usual in these scenarios, just as we were thinking of leaving, someone said, 'Sure, let's try a small bit longer.' The wind had dropped and the sky darkened, making a deadened, contrast-less, surreal scene. We saw some Minke whales, and though I repeatedly swam about trying to get in their paths, perhaps four or five hundred metres from the RIB, it was futile; back at the boat the lads were hysterical with laughter, telling me that the Minkes had kept swimming under the RIB. I gave up.

Turning for home, I saw some large fins travelling slowly in the water, the unmistakable sideways finning of a basking shark, possibly even two. We killed the engine and I slipped into the

Basking shark in a courtship ritual west of Clare

water, swimming the last couple of hundred of metres. The sea was thick with plankton, and I thought, 'I know what's going on here, sure I'll get a couple of shots at least.'

The sharks swam past me, first a couple, then more, and then more again, all huge animals, perhaps eight metres long, three layers deep and moving almost in formation. It was like a train in a scene from a children's animation film, where seemingly endless carriages bank around and around an unrealistically long curve in the landscape. When would it pass? And after a bit it dawned on me, the sharks were circling, the plankton was so thick I couldn't see the other side of what was probably a 20-metre-wide circle. Round and round they went: this was unlike anything I'd ever encountered; I'd never even seen a basking shark underwater without its mouth open, their heads looked so different this way.

The author and basking sharks in a courtship ritual west of Clare

As a cameraman, your first instinct is to shoot as well as you can and document the scene; in the water you might get one chance to film a passing shark or whale, a few short seconds, and your focus, exposure, composition etc. better all be good. But this was the most improbable of scenes. I'd never been so close to so many basking sharks. As they drifted gracefully through the water I could see all the exquisite detail of the pigmentation on their skin, their moving, inquisitive eyes, and most of the animals bearing scars from cookiecutter shark bites, Tasmanian devil-like animals that rise from the deep, take a cookie-sized bite and disappear again: what a way to make a living.

The sharks kept coming, all with lamprey eels – sometimes several – attached mostly behind their pelvic fins, near the reproductive organs. At times it was difficult to tell the males' claspers apart from the eels, but this clearly was the sheltered spot favoured by the eels – less drag, I guess, though not great for the sharks.

As staggering as it was to witness this scene, it was only later, when viewing Kev Smith's drone shots, that we realised the uniqueness of the gathering. Kev is an amazing, skilled, brave cameraman. I asked him to come into the water and try to get some underwater shots of me with the sharks. It was only later in a question-and-answer session at a college screening of the documentary, that I realised what I had actually asked him to do. Someone asked who'd filmed me and Kev put his hand up.

'Yeah I'd never swum in water that deep (100 metres) or so far offshore or with a shark, never mind sixteen of them. Ken's going, "Come on, come on, get closer, you have to shoot the detail" and I'm looking at these eight-metre sharks and my swim momentum is taking me right into their line, I'm trying to back up and he's going, come in closer ...'. The crowd were in hysterics and I felt like a right selfish eejit.

I'd noticed there was an even mix of males and females and that the males' claspers, where they hold their sperm, were swollen, but I still hadn't quite figured out what the sharks were doing: could it be courtship? Kev went researching and found something to suggest it could be a mating or pre-mating ritual. I did some more reading and emailed Professor David Simms in the UK, the world expert on basking sharks, who replied in a matter of minutes. This was to become an important moment in our understanding of the animals.

Researchers had seen the circling activity from an aircraft in Canada in 1998, and shark hunters had reported similar activity off Cornwall in the 1940s and '50s, but as no one had been in the water and hence been able to identify the sexes, this was likely the first documented instance of basking shark courtship behaviour. Of course, without seeing actual copulation, we can never be 100 per cent sure. I could have stayed longer in the water though I felt the half hour I was with the sharks was enough, and disturbing them was the last thing I'd want to do, but it's difficult to think of another reason for the shark's behaviour. On viewing the video footage, David Simms was hugely enthusiastic and set about writing a research paper on the activity. Later that summer, some scuba divers photographed similar activity just north of where we were, and in a similar water depth, so we can now say that this area is an important habitat for basking sharks, but huge gaps remain in our knowledge of these animals and consequently our ability to protect them.

My sightings of bird and whale activity transpired to be along what is known as a coastal front, an area where cold, nutrient-rich water wells up from the deep, bringing fertility, plankton blooms, small fish and ensuing predators from blue sharks to seals, birds to numerous whale species and on this day, basking sharks.

Basking sharks were hunted for at least two hundred years in Ireland: their livers, which take up almost a third of their body, made a highly valued and versatile oil. Coastal communities hunted them and it was said that their oil could light a whole village for a year and indeed there was a time when the streets

Freediving with basking sharks

of Dublin and Cork were lit with basking-shark oil. In later times their oil was used in cosmetics and even aeronautical engineering, as its consistency remains the same under fluctuating pressure levels when other oils coagulate.

9,000 sharks were killed in the Achill Island station alone between 1940 and 1954, and it appears Norwegian boats hunted them in EU and Irish waters until as recently as 2006. The basking shark of the northeast Atlantic is listed as Vulnerable in the International Union for Conservation of Nature (IUCN) Red List and is included in the OSPAR list of threatened or declining species and in Appendix II of the Convention on International Trade in Endangered Species (CITES).

In Ireland wild animals are protected under the 1976 Wildlife Act, but for some odd reason, this act excludes marine fish and invertebrates, meaning that legally these creatures are not classified as 'wildlife'. Basking sharks being fish (the second-largest in the world after whale sharks) are therefore a legally unprotected species in Irish waters, although it is illegal to land them, and under EU law it is forbidden to target-fish them. Clearly, much more needs to be done to conserve basking sharks in Ireland.

BUBBLE-NET FEEDING

WHAT WE SEE of whales from above the ocean surface in the barest of moments they spend there is, without doubt, a minuscule insight into the lives of these fascinating creatures; but perhaps no more so than what a whale would make of humans, having observed us flapping about underwater in the short amounts of time we are able to spend there.

I tried for many, many years to encounter whales underwater around Ireland, so as to observe and document what they do, which in Irish waters is mainly feeding and resting. But humans swimming with whales and dolphins is generally not a great idea: in my experience, more often than not, whales try to avoid us and go to some lengths to do so. Most cetacean scientists are opposed to humans swimming with whales and dolphins and, broadly, though not exclusively, I agree with them. Whales and dolphins spend their lives feeding, breeding and resting in between migrating between the places where they do all of this. These are their life functions, at least what we currently know of them.

I tried for many years to film a humpback whale feeding in Ireland, from underwater – not because I wanted a buzz (or that currently popular term to 'tick my bucket list'), but because I wanted to understand and document what happens.

Humpbacks lunging up through a bubble net west of Kerry

Bubble-net feeding is a truly amazing behaviour to observe, yet we still don't fully understand how these clever, enormous animals do it. In essence, swimming after a shoal of fish is somewhat ineffective, even with a mouth as enormous as a humpback's, since the fish can swim just as fast if not faster than a whale. So the humpbacks somehow figured out a way to 'trap' the shoals by

blowing air bubbles in a circle from underwater, forming a kind of tunnel or curtain as the bubbles rise to the surface. The fish are reluctant to swim through the bubbles so when the whale rises up through the curtain with its mouth wide open, their only escape is upwards onto the sea surface, where the humpback simply scoops them up.

Several humpbacks will often work cooperatively on this; it's fascinating to see how the technique is passed on between animals, though perhaps for the whales it's quite obvious, especially when you're hungry. I listened to BBC documentaries claiming that this had only ever been observed in Alaska, whilst I watched it for many years off the coasts of Cork and Kerry.

To my knowledge the only time bubble-net feeding had ever been filmed underwater was with a National Geographic Critter-cam in Alaska. This is where scientists attach a remote camera onto a whale's back; the camera shoots continuously, eventually detaches and the guys pick it up and recover the footage. With this set-up the camera angle gives the whale's point of view, so you see the fish and other whales but not necessarily the actual bubble-net feeding.

But I knew that if it could be filmed by a person, a cameraman under the water, then he could decide what to film, how to compose shots and move the camera around to document all the facets and mechanisms of this feeding activity, and also use his observations to describe these later. As there are gaps in our understanding of humpbacks, it would be a hugely useful achievement. Still, there's a reason why no one has swum up to these 35-tonne animals and attempted to film them chasing their prey in the cold temperate and Arctic waters where they feed with water visibility under five metres, I suppose.

We'd filmed bubble-net feeding with drones and from our RIB many times over the years, and studied the animals' movements to try and understand how I might do it safely and without disturbing the whale. I'd entered the water a few times near a bubble net, but it all happens so quickly, especially with two humpbacks working together, that I was never able to get close enough to see the action.

~~~~~~~~

But today feels different. It's November and I'm in the water twenty kilometres from land, swimming towards where I hope a single humpback will rise. Not so much swimming, with my arms occupied pushing a three-stone camera in front of me, but kicking with leg fins for propulsion. I've always felt these giant one-metre freedive fins were cumbersome and slow, though it's all down to anaerobic fitness, how the All Blacks used to beat other rugby teams, by training full time – lung-bursting, relentless, stop-start anaerobic attrition.

Today though, I'm terrified these fins are moving me too fast. I've swum a couple of hundred metres from the RIB and I know the humpback isn't far away, the lads back in the boat have been pointing straight ahead of me, they're too far to hear, but there's an awful inevitability about now ... I've waited, trained, thought about what happens next, dreamed and dreaded. I see the bubbles rise, I have a decision to make, so vulnerable, am I mad? A tiny breakable creature in an alien world trying to film a giant a hundred times my size, the weight of six adult elephants, a monster chasing his prey, and I want to film it.

This is a path I followed long ago, and a sense of obligation to my years of work and instinct to trust – well, my instinct, leads me on and in a flash, I'm back searching for the dark figure, trying to observe the shape of the bubble ring so as to keep myself outside it. As the bubbles intensify, the sprat come flying up, some spilling through gaps, and though all of this happens in three seconds, it seems an age as I take it all in … the frantic sprat movement triggers the realisation that there are no other animals here, where have all the common dolphins and diving birds gone? In that moment I understand they know better than to risk being here. Stupid human.

The humpback's five-metre pectoral fins fly through the water, dancing a delicate, pre-rehearsed move and lifting the animal the last few metres to the water's surface, its mouth opens as the gargantuan throat pleats balloon out. No photograph can do justice to the scale of what's happening in front of me. I'm terrified, but my focus is to just keep the camera composed. In a single arcing movement, the animal gulps a 40-tonne mouthful of water and I sense its direction before it dives and propel myself and my camera through the bubble net, vainly trying to stay close as it sweeps past me, contracting its enormous mouth to squeeze out the seawater and gollop the sprat.

Only on watching the video later do I realise that the whale tucks in its pectoral fin to avoid me, or perhaps that's just the optimum way for it to dive. There's so much we still don't know.

Gone.

Humpback whale diving after bubble-net feeding

It takes a few moments to make some sense of what's just happened. In a heightened sense of awareness we can observe and rationalise things at lightning speed, but often a second wave of slower thought process and absorption follows. I've done it. I've filmed a humpback whale bubble-net feeding, here in Ireland's winter Atlantic waters, I'm all right, I didn't disturb the animal, I think I've filmed it OK. An enormous wave of relief sweeps over me.

The lads in the boat are pointing again; now emboldened, I chase to another hunt. Bubbles rise and again, the only animals here are the sprat and the whale ... and me. This time the humpback rises from left to right, I time my swimming momentum to take me in through the bubbles and close to the animal, following its movement and staying just far enough away to avoid impact. But nature doesn't follow even lines – curves and crookedness and unpredictability are the beautiful textures and chaos of our natural world. Humpbacks blow the bubbles in spurts from deeper water as they're circling and rising, and so there are gaps and then sometimes super-concentrated streams of bubbles.

Peering through a gap and getting close, I try to align my motion and direction with the moving whale, only entering the bubble net after the animal has gulped its shoal of prey; hopefully not disturbing it, I swim into a geyser-like spring of bubbles much thicker than anything I've seen so far, gravity had delayed its rise into my path … I'm blinded and my momentum is taking me forward. Although the whale has mostly passed, the tail fin at the end of its 15-metre body sweeps out at me through the mass of bubbles within a foot of my camera, blanketed with barnacles,

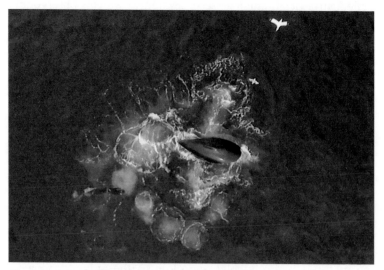

Entering into the bubble net as the whale dives

and it's funny how my first thought is of pirates supposedly 'keel-hauling' men under their ship as punishment, scraping their bodies over the barnacle-encrusted hull.

In an instant the animal has passed and is diving. I kick with everything I have and dive after it, trying to continue the video sequence, and in a moment of luck I end up just deep enough to capture the underside of its tail fluke; I can see a distinctive black spot and some other lines on the mostly white fluke.

~~~~~~

Pádraig Whooley, who collates the humpback catalogue at the IWDG, later tells me that this animal is HBIRL24, number 24 in the Irish catalogue. The number sounds cold, missing something that might describe the creature – but these are facts, and cute

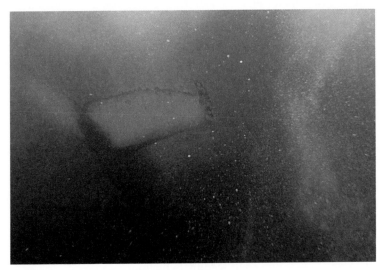

HBIRL24 diving after a feeding lunge

names for wild animals are misrepresentative of them. Science must be solid and unemotive, though perhaps not exclusively so.

It transpires that the amazingly dedicated whale researcher Nick Masset has photographed HBIRL24 around the Blasket Islands during each of the last four years, including six times the previous summer. In fact, we went on to photograph another four humpbacks in this area, which Pádraig painstakingly matched, by eye, to other photographs of the same animals taken in previous years off Cork and Kerry, three of them off the Blaskets by Nick.

This is a wonderful development but leads us to ascertain that there is a new pattern in humpback-whale feeding behaviour here in Irish waters. Since about 2003 humpbacks had shown up off the south coast, mainly Cork, but also Wexford and Waterford in early winter, feeding on sprat and herring that spawn around that time. A fish about to spawn is rich and fatty and a bountiful catch. Fishermen refer to fish that have already spawned as 'spent'. I once caught a pollack with a spent herring in its mouth, a withered, anaemic-looking creature. So it's somewhat amazing that humpbacks, as well as other whale species, dolphins, seabirds, tuna, seals and even sharks can time their arrival into areas of the ocean to coincide with aggregating and spawning fish.

I sent this underwater footage to humpback-whale scientists in Alaska who have studied humpbacks and bubble-net feeding for over twenty years; they had used the Crittercam, but never seen the view I was able to shoot, or indeed had the benefit of my observations. I hope my footage will contribute to our knowledge of these animals and their feeding behaviour.

There's no doubt that the dive was a potentially very dangerous thing to do, but it was not something I undertook lightly. I spent years working out how I might execute it safely and without interfering with the whale's feeding, and believe I eliminated as much risk as possible.

But would I do it again? Hmm.

~~~~~~

Nick Masset spends days sitting on a headland in West Kerry, watching the ocean through a spotting scope. While I've done a fair bit myself I would never have Nick's patience, and his research has been invaluable in documenting dozens of individual humpback whales in Ireland, which both he and Pádraig Whooley have, through hours of staring at hundreds of humpback images, managed to match to different locations, building up patterns of where these animals are seen and how they behave.

Humpbacks come to Ireland to feed, and in late winter migrate south to their tropical breeding grounds, journeys of 4,000 to 7,000 km each way. The animals don't feed in the tropics or during these journeys, and so face up to five months without food, meaning they need to put on a serious amount of fat whilst on their feeding grounds in order to sustain them for their impending journeys.

A few years ago Nick began identifying humpback whales off Kerry from summer through to autumn and matched individuals with those seen off Cork in early winter. A definite pattern emerged: summer feeding on sprat and sand eels along the rich coastal front around the Blasket Islands, then winter feeding in the Celtic Sea off the south coast on spawning sprat and herring.

The numbers of animals in the Irish humpback whale catalogue went from six to about seventy-eight in just fifteen years. A great conservation story of a seemingly recovering whale population, but all was not quite as well as it seemed.

Colin Barnes is a former fisherman and now a whale-watch operator in West Cork. Colin knows more about whales and their feeding behaviour that anyone else I've ever met – I guess near forty years on the sea actually observing these animals and their associated habitats and prey fish will get you to that level of knowledge and understanding.

Colin observed incessant pair-trawling for sprat in the Celtic Sea off Cork, two fishing trawlers dragging a net between them and around the shoals of spawning sprat. Over several years the massive shoals of these fish declined more and more, almost mirroring the nineteenth-century collapse of the once-great pilchard fishery that had enriched Baltimore and its people.

For almost ten years Colin, the IWDG, the Irish Wildlife Trust, BirdWatch Ireland and many more NGOs and individuals including myself, raised the issue with the authorities, the responsible government minister and his related officialdom, pleading for an end to the pair-trawling of sprat.

Although once popular for human consumption, sprat are regarded as not significantly commercially viable, or at least not enough to justify a fishing quota or total allowable catch, and there is currently no management plan for sprat in the seas around Ireland. So sprat can be fished more or less endlessly, until of course the inshore stocks deplete as they have done. Their price varies, in recent years it fluctuated between €150 and €200 per tonne, compared to say mackerel at €1,000 a tonne. I'm led to believe that much of the sprat is ground into fish meal for fish farms, and some is even used as lawn fertiliser.

Sprat are a vital constituent part of the marine ecosystem; feeding on zooplankton, they are an essential link in converting plankton into fish. A myriad of larger fish, whales, dolphins, sharks, tuna and dozens of species of seabirds consume sprat. Crucially, they are also prey for herring, a stock already massively depleted, and hence taking vast quantities of them out of the ocean, particularly at the time when they are reproducing, is a bad idea.

Conor Ryan carried out research over several years, which showed that sprat are the most important prey species for humpback whales in the Celtic Sea off Ireland's south coast, and the second most important prey species for fin whales, the second-largest animal ever to have lived. Conor took skin and blubber samples from feeding whales and, using a method known as stable isotope analysis, was able to track 'markers' in the whale skin, which identified on what fish species the animals had been feeding. But then, Colin Barnes had been telling us this for ten years, and indeed I had seen this again and again with my own eyes, filming whales under and over water, but Conor's research was intractable scientific evidence.

And so, in the winter of 2016, no humpbacks showed in the Celtic Sea off Cork for the first time in fifteen years, and indeed the same was true the following winter. During the same period we were able to document some of the same whales who usually fed off Cork at that time, appearing and feeding for the first time ever on sprat almost 300 km to the north, off Clare, in October and November. Why would these animals make such a dramatic change to their feeding habits?

It was with utter disbelief that, at the end of 2016, we came to hear of a new sprat fishery being opened to the west of Kerry and Clare.

I understand that by 2018 just a tiny number of humpbacks had been seen off Cork for the third consecutive winter. Although weather conditions have prohibited extensive time at sea, I myself have had no definite sightings of humpback whales off Clare over these last two winters, which begs the question: where did they go?

I've been told by fisheries officials that there is no problem with sprat in these waters. And these same officials have said that no surveys or population estimates or basic ecological studies (such as when exactly spawning occurs) have been carried out for sprat in these same inshore waters. In fact, it is currently unknown whether there are even different stocks of sprat in these areas.

The International Council for the Exploration of the Sea (ICES) provides non-biased, non-political scientific advice to member nation governments and international regulatory commissions.

A 2015 ICES report[1] stated that in regard to sprat in Irish waters: 'The stock structure of sprat populations in this ecoregion is not clear ... There is insufficient information to evaluate the status of sprat in this area. Another ICES report[2] also from 2015 stated: 'ICES advises that when the precautionary approach is applied, catches should be no more than 3500 tonnes in each of 2016 and 2017.'

Actual catch for these areas around Ireland in 2015 was 10,368 tonnes[3] with 9,332 tonnes by Irish vessels and the rest by non-Irish vessels.

In 2016 the sprat catch was 6,882 tonnes[3,4] (4,763 tonnes by Irish vessels) and in 2017 figures are only available for Irish vessels, which was 4,260 tonnes[4], almost the same as the Irish 2016 total, so we can broadly estimate that total catch was similar to 2016's 6,882 tonnes, almost twice the ICES recommendation.

So in these years, documented catches of sprat have been two to three times above the ICES recommended level.

A new ICES document on sprat referenced in the Marine Institute's *Stock Book 2017* states that 'Catches (of sprat) should be no more than 2,800 tonnes in each of the years 2018 and 2019.' ICES research documents on sprat repeatedly state, almost to a comical level, that 'Irish data may be underestimated, due to difficulties in quantifying the landings from vessels of less than 10 m length.'

---

1   ICES HAWG REPORT 2015, section 10, p. 637

2   ICES Advice on fishing opportunities, catch, and effort, Celtic Seas Ecoregion. Published 30 June 2015

3   ICES Sprat stock advice 2017 (DOI:10.17895/ices.pub.3258)

4   The Stock Book 2018, Marine Institute

As I understand it, vessels under a certain size are not required to report catch levels. The situation has been compounded by the recent and dramatic decline in herring in these same waters, often fished by the same vessels and fishermen. The herring stock to the west and north of Ireland collapsed to such a degree that there is a zero TAC (catch) from 2018. To the south, the Celtic Sea herring stock has recovered after areas had been closed to fishing from the 1970s, but the fishery again collapsed in 2018.

In mid-2018 the current government minister responsible for fisheries finally opened a consultation process on fisheries in inshore waters, albeit with a view to potentially limiting fishing vessel sizes within a six-mile limit of the coast, but this might possibly include activities such as pair-trawling for sprat in inshore waters.

Then finally, just before Christmas 2018, more than ten years after Colin Barnes and others had raised this issue, after over eight hundred submissions were received by the minister responsible for fisheries, it was announced that trawlers above 12 metres were to be prohibited from fishing within an area six miles from the coast, and specifically sprat fishing was to be phased out over three years although there is no guideline catch level for 2019, which is somewhat worrying. Currently there are claims of industry reluctance to accede to these measures and reports of political lobbying.

I genuinely applaud the minister and his officials for taking this action. I believe in trying to bring about change by working with people, creating awareness, encouraging stakeholders rather than firing bullets. While it's easy to just point fingers and especially post or share bad news on social media, it's vastly more difficult and time-consuming to actually work with stakeholders to achieve positive change.

In Australian waters there are several stocks of humpback whales, and in places the numbers of some had fallen to perhaps just a few thousand by the 1970s. The Aussies take ocean con-servation seriously, and measures were brought in to protect and study these particular whales. Today there are estimated to be in the region of 30,000 humpbacks visiting those areas.

Granted, Australian waters are enormous compared to Ireland's, but we can ponder this story before self-congratulating on figures of one or even two hundred humpbacks visiting Ireland to feed, constituting a recovery to pre-whaling levels.

CLAHANE – SPRING TIDE

I walked across the dewy grass
Scrunchy beneath my boots
Now not so clean but another day's work
Perhaps, some laden purity to be attained.
My gaze across the open bay
Was dazzled now myopically
By the petting excited gallery
That fringed the line between land and sea
Beneath me
Like a small theatre orchestra
Almost buried beneath stage and folk
But bellowing and aurally posturing.
Trundling barrel-bellied salt water
Flattered by gaseous applause
Made frontal attack on the limestone-thighed
Shoreline
Indifferent somehow, by now
Waiting, the latent partner in an arranged marriage.

BURREN FIELD

Across the valley, a golden field
Is lovingly lit in a late evening
Summer sun
Beaming rows of fresh cut hay, lay
Obediently across the now golden stub
Baby swallows dance provocatively
Around each other
Perhaps swashbucklingly jubilant
At their early discovery of this kingdom.
And distantly, I wonder if I am better to
Embrace their place
Or admire and dream from far away.

JOURNEY TO THE DEEP

THE DEEP SEABED is an area thought of for thousands of years as a deep, dark, lifeless abyss. Where there can be no light, there can be no life, or so the thinking goes. Yet stories abound, especially among seamen, of giant octopus and other sea monsters cowering in the deep and waiting to pounce on any able-bodied seaman unfortunate enough to end up overboard, for an end such a plight would surely be. I can recall a movie scene I watched as a child, of a scuba diver being attacked by a giant octopus, all eight arms covered in horrible suckers, wrapping and enfolding the unfortunate struggling diver, even slithering across his dive mask and eyes … the diver draws a knife, but it's useless against so many tentacles … as death dawns, the human thinks of one last desperate move, and lunges with the knife at the animal's brain, 'The ink, the ink,' one of my older siblings called out, 'they're full of black ink, that must be their weak spot,' and the punctured octopus immediately loosens its grip on the now victorious diver, darkness yet again conquered by man.

Octopus, like most all wild creatures, at least in my experience of them, tend to flee on any sight of humans.

I guess such lack of knowledge – or ignorance, to give it its true name – was somewhat understandable in the time before we understood the nature and diversity of life in the deep ocean. It was also perhaps part of the reasoning as to why countries dumped their radioactive waste here in the deep ocean, into this dark, empty, lifeless abyss, five kilometres deep, and where it would surely never be seen again.

From the 1940s up until 1983, European countries dumped this kind of waste in the Northeast Atlantic, to the south and west of Ireland. According to figures I've seen, Britain was the greatest culprit, dumping 75,000 tonnes, which is estimated to be 78 per cent of the total European amount.

Large amounts of the dumping work in the north-east Atlantic were contracted out to private vessels, and captains would be told they'd have limited exposure time to the radiation, perhaps 72 hours, before it became dangerous. There are stories of bad weather and panicking or perhaps unscrupulous sailors dumping the waste much closer to land than they were contracted to do. A Cornish seaman told me he recalled a barrel of radioactive waste washing up on the south Cornwall coast during a 1970s winter storm.

Records are deliberately inconclusive, with some British documents having details blacked out. I saw an interview with Michael Meacher, the former British Environment Minister, where he talked about this, though it happened long before his time in power. He felt – although he had no direct evidence – that the dumping had been a cooperative action undertaken or facilitated by the military to solve a 'national problem', and of course British Nuclear Fuels, the state-owned power generation company, were likely at the centre of this.

It happened all across the planet: Russia and the former USSR also dumped similar amounts in the Atlantic, Pacific and even Arctic waters and there are legions of stories of American dumping of radioactive waste in both the Pacific and the North Atlantic deep ocean areas. United States Environmental Protection Agency records indicate that more than 55,000 containers of radioactive wastes were dumped at three ocean sites in the Pacific Ocean between 1946 and 1970. Almost 34,000 containers of radioactive wastes were dumped at three ocean sites off the US East Coast from 1951 to 1962. (Source https://www.epa.gov/ocean-dumping/learn-about-ocean-dumping#Before). In several cases former navy sailors were contracted in to do this work, many not even understanding what was in the barrels they rolled overboard by hand.

When there was a Government in Somalia, it's alleged they accepted payment from some European countries in return for the dumping of nuclear waste in Somalian waters, there are even allegations of involvement by the Italian Mafia. When the Somalian government collapsed, these waters became a convenient place to dispose of European nuclear waste, which of course could now be done 'free of charge'. Foreign fishing fleets also joined in the bounty of restriction-free fishing in a country without government or ability to defend itself and its waters – the story of the Somali pirate is not quite as simple as some would have us believe. During the 2004 Indian Ocean tsunami barrels of radioactive waste washed ashore along some coastlines and there are incidents of unexplained child deformities among coastal communities.

Greenpeace activists trying to stop the dumping of radioactive waste in the North Atlantic in the 1980s. The barrels were dropped onto the RIB, smashing it and throwing the driver into the sea dangerously close to the ship propellers. It became a seminal moment in the fight to stop the dumping at sea, with a global outcry when it made international news coverage. We used video footage of this incident in Ireland's DEEP ATLANTIC *to tell the story of the dumping.*

~~~~~~~

It's impossible to define what we might refer to as deep; is it ten or a thousand metres? Us humans, once we reach beyond a depth where we can stand up and still breathe, feel we're in deep water. To the west of Ireland, the seabed of the North Atlantic is on average about 200 metres below the water surface, then between 70 and 200 km out, depending on which part of the coast you measure, there are underwater cliffs that fall off dramatically, first to 2,000, then 3,000 and ultimately to 5,000 metres below the ocean surface, to an area called the Abyssal Plain. All of this drop-off is known as the edge of the continental shelf, the continent being that of mainland Europe. In some places the drop off to 2,000 metres happens in just a few kilometres – think of the Cliffs of Moher multiplied by ten.

The Victorians were true innovators in scientific research, and so much of what we now know is based on their early research efforts. In 1872 the British ship HMS *Challenger* set sail on a four-year scientific research expedition, one of the first of its kind, covering 130,000 km around the globe. The team of scientists on board made hundreds of mid- and deep-water trawls and for the first time ever, refuted the notion that life could not exist beyond, say, a depth of five hundred metres, as they collected thousands of species of flora and fauna new to human knowledge, including deep-water coral. This, of course, was almost a hundred years before the dumping of radioactive waste in the deep ocean, so the good folks who decided on that strategy knew a little more than they may have claimed to.

As technology advanced, our ability to reach the deep seabed increased and scientific allegation grew of even more life in this, the darkest part of our planet. Ironically, some of this was led by fisheries. By the 1970s, as fish stocks were declining from over-exploitation, fishermen in the Southern Ocean, particularly around New Zealand and Australia, began trawling over the seamounts and canyons of the deep ocean, some more than a thousand metres deep. They discovered a bounty of fish, a new frontier to be reaped. Many of these areas, it later transpired, were grounds where fish aggregated in huge groups to mate and spawn.

By the early 1990s European trawlers began fishing seamounts in the deep Atlantic to the west of Ireland, followed by Irish trawlers around the millennium. The orange roughy is a deep-water fish that can live for 150 years. It is slow growing and late maturing, making it vulnerable to over-exploitation, but it has tasty flesh and fetched a good market price. It was fished almost exclusively by bottom trawling, a hugely invasive fishing method of dragging metal plates along the deep seabed and canyons to disturb everything on the seabed, which is then captured within the attached net. By-catch of unwanted or unsuitable fish species, crustaceans, cold-water coral and a myriad of other life forms is enormous but part of the 'accepted' collateral damage. I've seen disturbing photos of trawl marks across cold water-coral reefs.

The orange roughy was another new frontier, but within a few short years catches began to dramatically decline – scientists began research efforts to understand the stock, but before they could get to a point of recommending less fishing, the stock had

Orange roughy catch. PHOTO: MARK LEWIS

more or less collapsed in parts of the north-east Atlantic, just as it had done in the Southern Ocean a few years previously. There would have been individual orange roughy fish alive from the time US president Abraham Lincoln abolished slavery in the 1860s until Barack Obama became US president in 2008, and yet these same fish were almost wiped out in just ten years of fisheries.

After twelve or thirteen years spent documenting life in the shallow seas around Ireland, mainly scuba diving on my own with my camera, I became fascinated by the new frontier of the deep ocean. I wanted to understand what forms of life lived there, how they could survive, and equally interestingly, if or how life on the deep seabed was connected to other life in the surface waters of the deep ocean. My dream was to make this into a television documentary series.

Even the most technical scuba diver can only dive to a paltry 100-metre depth, so the challenge of how to get a camera down to 3,000 metres to explore and document life in those areas is considerable.

I had been in conversation with the Irish Marine Institute since 2009 when we covered a piece on Dr Anthony Grehan from NUI Galway and his pioneering work in documenting cold-water coral reefs in Irish shelf-edge waters, many for the first time. Anthony's efforts were hugely successful in helping to conserve some of these areas where the first coral reefs were discovered.

But I wanted to get to these areas myself and be a part of the research, to have access to the cameras and to film the life that is to be found here. I was extremely fortunate, then, to be invited to take part in several research expeditions to the deep Atlantic on board *Celtic Explorer*.

Explorer is an amazing state-of-the-art floating research facility with diesel–electric engines, quiet enough not to scare fish so as to carry out unobtrusive and therefore more accurate research. It has a Remotely Operated Vehicle (ROV), *Holland 1*, which can dive

Celtic Explorer *on her way to the deep ocean*

to 3,000 metres with half-a-dozen cameras on board, lights, two robotic arms to gather samples and an underwater hoover to suck mud samples from the seabed. There is a wet lab for analysing and processing samples of fish and other life taken from the ocean, and a dry lab with the most up-to-date computing technology. *Explorer* is capable of doing everything from operating as a full-blown fishing trawler for annual fisheries surveys to hosting and launching the ROV, and mapping the seabed on transatlantic voyages. I've been on board when they were laying an underwater cable from land to bring electricity and fibre-optic internet connectivity to an open-ocean research platform. It's even capable of making its own drinking water from the sea. The ship never seems to spend more than 36 hours turning around in port, readying for its next expedition and is at sea for an incredible 330 days a year, making it Europe's busiest research ship.

In 2015 I was invited to accompany Professor Andy Wheeler from University College Cork on a trip to Porcupine Bank, 300 km west of Ireland. RTÉ had commissioned and backed the documentary project, but I didn't yet have all the funding required to make a project as challenging as this. In the era of declining broadcaster revenue, it's very difficult to get ambitious documentary projects funded, particularly in a country as small as Ireland.

Our main funding decision was due about the time of Andy's voyage and so I decided to go anyway, as this was a one-off opportunity, although without a budget I would have to do everything myself, camera, sound, directing and even presenting. Andy is a brilliant man, a pioneering deep-sea geologist. His expeditions are a joy, as he encourages and empowers those around him, especially young students, many at sea for the first time. Being at sea for any length of time can be tricky – it's a rather unreal situation, even on a 65-metre vessel like *Explorer*, and although you have all the luxuries of food, comfortable cabins, even satellite TV, it's still a somewhat confined space to spend two to three weeks with limited sleep and constant shift work.

We embarked from Galway docks through the lock gates, opened only for an hour either side of high tide, and I got an early indication of the skills and seamanship of the ship's crew as they manoeuvred the vessel through the lock channel with what seemed less than a metre to spare on either side, I'd have been nervous driving our 8-metre RIB through a gap that tight, never mind a 65-metre ship.

In no time we were steaming south west and everyone was excited, many of us meeting for the first time: there was a real buzz and I felt a part of something special. I would be documenting their research work, much of it innovative and important, and bringing it to the living rooms of Ireland via RTÉ.

Less than an hour out to sea, my phone rang: it was my wife Katrina, in tears, telling me that the funding decisions had been released and her documentary project, which she'd worked on for three years at that stage, had been refused. 'Check your email,' she told me, 'you may have better news.' I checked, only to discover that I had also been turned down. I was heading to sea for two weeks with a group of scientists and a ship's crew who didn't know me but whose work I had promised to document for a TV series, which now wasn't going to happen. As I called Katrina back, I glanced at the pier wall at Rossaveal, just three miles away and fleetingly felt the urge to jump in and swim. But I couldn't do that. I consoled Katrina as much as I could, and she me. We'll fight on, we said, we'll manage somehow.

I went to my cabin, pulled the curtains and sat on the bed, I wanted to lock out the world. Apart from anything else, I didn't know how we'd manage to subsist for the foreseeable future. How would I support our family, pay the mortgage? Even beginning another project would take at least a year to secure funding.

At such junctures you decide to fight or lie down. Thankfully I was able to gather some strength, and with emotion burning inside

Professor Andy Wheeler from University College Cork aboard Celtic Explorer, *June 2015*

me, I decided to stand up and fight – I'd get back to land and make a stronger application and show the funders this was important work, not just an entertaining TV series. We were producing vital footage for critical environmental and conservation matters and would match the BBCs of this world on a fraction of their budgets, all in an Irish context, and much of it for the first time ever.

I went to find Andy and told him what had happened, but that I was determined to fight on and realise this project. For someone who had only met me once, Andy Wheeler was surprisingly and immediately supportive. That evening I shot the first of Andy's interviews where he charismatically and with superb clarity explained the importance of the deep ocean to the world and what he and his team were trying to achieve with their research work: these pieces formed the bedrock of the deep ocean section for *Ireland's DEEP ATLANTIC*, which eventually secured funding in early 2016.

~~~~~~~~~

Explorer has berths for thirty-five people. The crew of eighteen consisted of the captain (or master as some call him), first mate, second mate, bosun, engineer and second engineer, cook and cook's helper, six ROV pilots who rotate on twelve-hour shifts and four able-bodied seamen. That leaves seventeen berths for research scientists and myself. Many of the scientists are undergraduates who've come along to gain experience and to carry out some of the more mundane aspects of research, such as water-sampling, logging and cataloguing life forms collected in the deep, or linear tubes of mud taken vertically from the seabed, which provide valuable information about climate changes over the thousands of years during which the sediment from where they were collected accumulated.

Some expeditions can accommodate a bird- and/or cetacean-watch person, who will dutifully climb to the crow's nest, the highest point on the ship, nine floors up from water level. As you ascend away from the water the ship's movement becomes more exaggerated, a bit like climbing up a metronome, since the further you are from the base, the more you swing. They then spend hours watching the open ocean through a pair of binoculars, truly nauseating work if there's any kind of sea swell, logging any encounters with birds, whales or dolphins. Nothing happens for 99.9 per cent of their time, then you'll hear an excited roar, '*Whale*! Nine o'clock!' probably similar to sailors of old spotting land. Funny how our outlook has changed.

So as to maximise deck and storage space, crew accommodation on most ships is built stacked in a kind of high-rise of up to six or seven stories of cabins, with perhaps three levels below deck. The lowest-ranked crewman's quarters are usually at the base below water level, and the captain's at the top. I find it ironic that in sea swell the captain therefore has the most uncomfortable location on board, but this is largely so that it is closest to the bridge, which by its nature requires the greatest panorama. Barry, the hugely amicable second mate on *Explorer*, told me how he served his time on cargo ships sailing the world. Once, while trying to sleep in a big storm, he calculated that his bunk – and therefore his head – was swinging thirty metres horizontally in either direction every ten seconds, gravity dragging the blood around his brain back and forth. I do prefer RIBs myself.

~~~~~~

There is a long history of drinking at sea, which I understand, given the monotony and isolation of the circumstance. Historically, naval sailors were given daily beer rations on the basis that fresh, clean water was difficult to acquire and store. In the days before modern water filtration, algae would flourish over long months at sea and stored water was easily contaminated – beer, however, would preserve well.

It appears that sometime in the eighteenth century the British navy replaced beer with rum: lower ranks would receive a daily watered-down dram of rum, and as one rose through the ranks, one's dram became stronger until at some point it was the full-blown 40 per cent alcohol version: sailors could even save up their rations and 'splice the main brace', a term still used by sailors to kick back and relax or celebrate. It's hard to believe this was standard practice by the British navy until 1970. Rum was sometimes diluted with water and lemon, which helped prevent scurvy, making the potion known as grog, from which the term groggy derives.

In fact it's fascinating how many sayings in our language derive from maritime life. Money for old rope, To give a wide berth, Batten down the hatches, Plain sailing, Run a tight ship, On board, Down in the doldrums, All at sea, High and dry, Sailing close to the wind, Three sheets to the wind, All hands on deck, Fire a shot across the bow, Learn the ropes, Loose cannon, Rock the boat – the list is somewhat endless and evidence of our long history of seafaring.

But the drinking culture at sea is no more, at least not on *Celtic Explorer*, which is a 'dry ship'. No alcohol allowed. I wondered about this as I prepared to board for a three-week expedition into the North Atlantic, I enjoy – though don't tend to crave – a drink, but the thought of total abstinence brought on little pangs of nervousness.

The ship is operated by P&O, the passenger ferry company, and perhaps because of this, there is a duty-free service on board. However, it only opens on the last day at sea when an orderly queue forms outside the captain's quarters, where you can buy spirits or cigarettes or even a *Celtic Explorer* T-shirt, all at hugely discounted prices. It seemed too good to miss. Mumbles were forthcoming about trust and the rule of not opening anything until standing back on dry land as we waited politely to acquire our contraband, the queue passing the ship's brig, a jail room which most every ship has and where an unruly crewman or passenger would be confined until return to port. I guess people did lose it at sea, and the danger of an out-of-control person was a great enough risk to the ship's safety to justify their confinement. I strongly suspect, though, that *Explorer*'s brig has yet to be occupied.

～～～～

We sailed southwest towards the Porcupine Seabight where the continental shelf first drops off from about 200 metres down to more than 2,000. Cruising at 12 knots, the journey would take a day. After some 'settling' time, you begin to feel the peacefulness of life at sea. I continually found myself out on deck absorbing the breathtaking panorama of the open ocean where cloud, sky and sea become a single canvas of varying shades of blues and whites. The ocean reflects the sky, and on very calm seas this vista becomes dimension-less, the blues blending into each other. On stormier days the drama boils with dramatic contrasts of colours, celestial light shooting between fleeting chinks in the restless clouds; *Explorer* pitches and rolls into and across the swell, waves smashing into her hull and morphing from a deep blue into gurgling, salty white water, rising up, up towards deck and slapping us with briny spray.

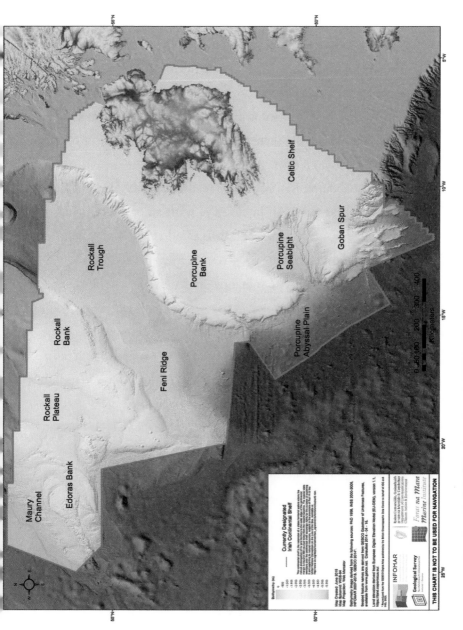

The real map of Ireland depicts the full extent of Ireland's marine territory and Exclusive Economic Zone of over 220 million acres (880,000 km²), which is ten times the size of the island of Ireland.

MARINE INSTITUTE AND GEOLOGICAL SURVEY IRELAND

Below deck the ship's cook, Jimmy, an effervescent Belfast man who's spent his life at sea, flies around the rocking kitchen, keeping about a dozen pans of all kinds of simmering food in check, all the time belting out Bon Jovi or Elton John in harmony with a radio, in fact his only pauses seem to be the reach a high note or chorus line: 'Let's go dooooooown, in a blaze of glory.'

'What about ye Kenny, are you really a coeliac?' 'Ah no Jimmy, I'm just wheat free.' 'Ah Jaysus, d'ye want an omelette?' and on seeing Jimmy's monstrous apple tarts smothered in runny custard, my wheat-free days were laid to rest, at least for this voyage.

As a child I had a romantic and cosy notion of being a stowaway on a transatlantic voyage, tucked up near to and kept warm by the ship's engine room. I wasn't to be disappointed as the low hum of *Explorer*'s diesel–electric engines soothed us into deep, dreamy sleep. The rise and fall and twists of the ocean surface are like most things in nature, uneven, but you eventually, perhaps subconsciously, discern a rhythm in ocean travel and relax into it.

Once I sailed through a stormy night off the south coast of England, trying to make it to Honfleur in northern France. The weather became dangerous and we doubled back for the shelter of the Isle of Wight, passing out of the stormy waters and motoring for the last few hours of passage. Sometime around dawn, as we approached safe anchorage in the lee of the island, I switched off the engine, and within moments all of my sleeping friends awoke.

~~~~~~~~

Andy and his team worked day and night, and by the time we'd reached the Porcupine Seabight they were ready to begin mapping the deep seabed from 3,000 metres above, as somewhat unbelievably there were no fine-detail maps for this area, or in fact for much of the world's deep seabed.

The ship has a technology known as multibeam sonar, essentially a way of mapping the seabed in three dimensions and thus documenting all of its cliffs, drop-offs, canyons, crevasses and myriad features. Andy and his guys would watch multiple computer screens, chatting in a language I didn't understand, pausing only when they hit some or other technical hitch. They'd think out loud, scratch heads, go quiet, confer but always come back with a solution. 'If we configured the multibeam in this way and then rendered the data in that way ...' etc. etc.

Once the maps were created they launched *Holland 1*. The first maps would guide it along the seabed, and the ROV, which had just had its own multibeam sonar installed, would then create the finest detailed maps ever of this area of the Atlantic, 'flying' just 100 metres above the deep seabed, locating and documenting previously unknown cold-water coral reefs.

When the ROV maps had been rendered and after multiple meetings with the captain and ship's crew and planning ROV dives lasting up to 24 hours, *Holland 1* was prepared again for launch. The amount of technology associated with the ROV is staggering: two shipping containers full of kit plus the ROV itself, all of which live in a warehouse near the Galway docks and are loaded painstakingly onto *Celtic Explorer* during her 36-hour window in port, and then unloaded on her return.

We sat expectantly in the ROV shack, a shipping container so full of technology and cameras that it made the bridge on *Star Trek* look sparse by comparison. It took an hour for *Holland 1* to reach the seabed 1,000 metres below us. You could have cut the air, such was the anticipation, and as the ROV pilots informed us we were now just 100 metres away it was so quiet I could hear myself swallowing.

And then from the blackness of the deep, a patch of pale gravelly seabed appeared, lit in an elliptical shape by the ROV lights – somewhat anti-climactic after all the work. The pilots flew the ROV perhaps another 100 metres across the seabed. Karl, a wonderfully-spirited American and long-time resident of West Cork said, glancing up at the navigation sonar, 'I think it's just up ahead' … and then out of the darkness appeared the most beautiful reef of cold-water coral, intricate, ornate, floral-shaped and multicoloured, surrounded by and supporting pristine white sponges and a myriad of other beautiful deep-ocean life forms.

The reef is formed by *Lophelia pertusa*, a coral skeleton made of calcium carbonate that grows incredibly slowly over thousands of years, it is occupied by soft polyps, separate and individual animals, which feed on passing plankton and bits of organic matter that the tidal currents sweep through here. As the coral dies away over time, new coral forms on its remains, this process slowly building mounds of coral hundreds of metres high over thousands of years and which ultimately then support an ecosystem of thousands of species of animals and plants.

Cold-water coral reef with sponge, anemones and other deep-ocean life forms

Over the following two weeks the ROV was constantly in the water; I watched the pilots perform amazing work flying *Holland 1* around the deep seabed, down through deep canyons and up the face of thousand-metre cliffs. Amazingly they can only see perhaps a few metres with the ROV's cameras and depend hugely on sonar images, a monochrome screen with a kind of hazy, impressionistic representation of seabed features, to actually see where they're going. As the weeks go on, the twelve-hour shifts demand more mugs of coffee … these men must need to sleep for a week when they get home.

After a while the dives began to become almost run of the mill as we all become familiar with the routine of launch and recovery of the ROV. Other 'guest' scientists get to have their time with the ROV and sit excitedly in the shack watching unfolding scenes 2,000 metres below us as animals and habitats they've spent much of their lives studying, usually in textbooks, appear before their eyes. Dr Agostina Vertino is an Italian marine scientist from the University of Milan and specialises in deep ocean geology and paleoecology – yes there is such a word, it's the study of a branch of ecology concerned with the characteristics of ancient environments and with their relationships to ancient plants and animals. This woman spends her life studying and trying to figure out how all these things are related. I do sometimes feel like a lightweight generalist when I meet people like Agostina with their brilliant minds and lifelong commitment to specialist research work.

During our expeditions Agostina found a species of cold-water coral common in the Mediterranean sea, which would later prove that the connectivity between the Med and the Atlantic was once much greater than it is now, through the tiny channel between Gibraltar and Spain. Agostina told me of finding *Lophelia pertusa* on a mountaintop in her native Sicily (in fact she had also found them on the walls of the cathedral in Palermo as the stone had been quarried from the same mountain). These were the same cold-water corals Andy was discovering in Irish waters and which can only live in deep water with a temperature of four degrees or less – meaning that the top of a mountain in Sicily was once at the bottom of a cold dark sea.

I showed Agostina fossils I'd photographed in Doolin and on Mullaghmore mountain in the Burren. Immediately recognising the fossil with an unpronounceable name, she smiled and told me yes these are very, very old you know, probably 300 million years and of course they could only live in shallow tropical seas, meaning that the Burren and my native Co. Clare were once much closer to the equator, even farther south than Sicily.

~~~~~~

Andy and his team discovered swathes of new areas of cold-water corals, all supporting thousands of species of flora and fauna, and all here in Irish waters, to the west of Cork and Kerry. Andy's scientific colleague, Dr Aaron Lim, a hugely amicable Cork man, told me they were likely looking at a full year to process all the video material, seabed and water samples and mapping data. In time all of this work and that of other *Explorer* expeditions will contribute to many of these deep-sea areas being designated as Special Areas of Conservation (SACs) where fishing and other human activities are prohibited.

After weeks at sea on the edge of the continental shelf, the captain turned *Explorer* back east and pointed her bow towards Galway. With too many night-long ROV sessions, staring bleary-eyed at arrays of video screens, I went for a very long and deep sleep, but for the scientists there was still endless work, cataloguing samples, backing up data, rendering maps etc. while the ship's crew began disassembling the ROV so as to shorten *Explorer*'s time in port and perhaps earn a few more sea hours for the next expedition.

I awoke after maybe fourteen hours' sleep to be greeted by the green waters of our inshore sea and the distant yet beautiful sight of the outer Blasket Islands, as Inis Tíreacht with its prehistoric

Ship's crew and scientists aboard Celtic Explorer, *June 2015*

pyramid outline came into sight. We were welcomed by pods of common dolphins, appearing giddy at our arrival with their ceaseless energy, and a small fishing trawler drawing lines of pollack on board and a mecca for what seemed like every seagull in West Kerry.

I wondered at the productivity of the ocean and how what we'd just seen on the deep seabed affected and impacted how these dolphins, whales, sea birds and thousands of other species of life, not to mention generations of coastal dwellers, survived on the bounty of the ocean.

I made three more trips to the deep ocean on *Celtic Explorer* over the following two years and managed to document some of the truly incredible and fertile life of these areas once thought to be an abyss and which Andy Wheeler calls 'the place of the devil'.

EXPLORING THE OPEN ATLANTIC

THROUGHOUT FOLKLORE I've found recurring references to mythical islands in the open Atlantic, usually lush with life and always somehow just beyond the reaches of discovery.

Hanging on my office wall is a sixteenth-century map of Europe by Abraham Ortelius, creator of the first atlas of the world. His map shows several islands to the south-west of Ireland, one titled St Brendain. In fact you'll find reference to Brendan's island on many maps; I've even seen one of the Azores mapped as Brendan's island and there is a bay in Iceland known locally as Brendan's Bay. Whether Brendan the navigator ever made it to North America we'll never know, but he and his hardy colleagues did make some brave and incredibly skilled sea journeys in their sixth-century cow-skin boat, encountering enormous whales, unspecified sea monsters and likely some serious Atlantic storms according to the Latin text documenting their journeys, the *Navigatio*. We know they made it to the Faroe Islands a journey of 1,200 km from West Kerry, and while there is some evidence of their presence in Iceland, the reality is that the journey was just a further 600 km, probably about a four-day sail. I've always been struck by that spirit of exploration and seamanship.

~~~~~~

The author at sea

In 2011 I was searching for humpback whales on a tiny RIB somewhere west of the Cape Verde islands, themselves 500 km west of Senegal, with whale scientist Dr Conor Ryan when we began discussing trying to get to the shelf edge to find large whales. This is a special place which begins 100km to the west of Ireland, the edge of the European continental shelf. Here the seabed drops dramatically from 200 down to 5,000 metres, and it's this change that creates an explosion of life. Plankton blooms, enormous shoals of fish, sharks, right up to blue and sperm whales, respectively the largest animal and largest predator ever to have graced planet Earth, they're all found here. Thousands of metres below them, deep-ocean squid, octopus, a myriad of crustacean species and literally hundreds of thousands of species of animals and plants inhabit the ocean bed, many of them centred along cold-water coral reefs.

In comparison to coastal seas, the open ocean is relatively barren, since nutrients and iron that are washed off the land don't reach this far offshore and the water is too deep for storms to churn them up from the seabed. So with no obvious fertility there is little for life to survive on, or so it seems. But life on our planet always somehow endures. Open-water fish, sharks, turtles, sea birds and most of all large whales, have survived and evolved through millions of years, adapting with some impressive survival behaviour and quite unbelievable migration journeys to find the places where they need to be.

～～～～～

I began researching the idea of making a documentary series on the deep waters of the North Atlantic around Ireland later in 2011 and made my first trip to the shelf edge on an angling charter boat that October. About forty miles out, we snagged a fishing rope around one of the propellers and couldn't dive to cut it off as the swell had risen and diving underneath the boat was too risky, so we had to turn and limp for home on one prop; it was a reminder of how things can so easily go wrong at sea.

I wasn't sure what we might encounter along the shelf edge, just that it felt like real exploration, and based on the explorer's oft naive belief that there is something great at the end of the journey.

Filming underwater is at the masochistic end of camerawork, at least in the North Atlantic, but filming in the coastal shallows,

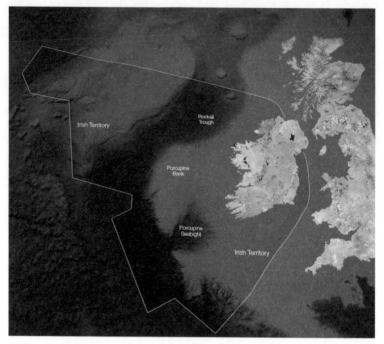

The open North Atlantic and the edge of the continental shelf to the west of Ireland. GRAPHIC: PHIL RAFFERTY

which is what I'd done for much of the previous ten years now seemed easy compared to trying to find and film a blue whale in the open North Atlantic, where there may be just a few or even none in an area of 10,000 km². And they can swim at 15–20 km per hour, near ten times what I can make pushing my enormous camera.

I spent several years researching, planning and most importantly, thinking about how we could realise this project. Raising funding for an ambitious film or TV production can be almost as much work as actually producing it, and with all of that unpaid time and effort, it's a risky business. But after two years we managed to get the money together and began shooting in spring 2016. RTÉ had hoped for delivery within a year, but understood it could take two.

We planned to make trips to the shelf edge in search of sperm and blue whales and possibly even some large sharks. A great part of this challenge was to use a vessel that could get you 70–100 km offshore, but also has the necessary speed to approach the fast-moving whales. A sailboat seemed ideal and very holistic, but it wouldn't have the required mobility. A RIB is perfect for that part, but driving 100 km offshore? I was extremely nervous about that.

With North Atlantic weather windows rare and unpredictable, our best-made plan was to try to sail to the shelf edge, bringing a small inflatable boat on board, but with deck space a constraint, we decided also to make some exploratory offshore trips by RIB while waiting for a 'sailing window'.

I couldn't afford a new RIB and so I bought a second-hand one, sold its single engine and bought two brand-new Honda outboards. Engine failure is your likeliest problem at sea, and fuel contamination is the likeliest problem with outboard engines. So we had the two new engines fitted, and built separate fuel tanks. (I only buy fuel from trusted sources, and even then I randomly test it with a specialist kit.)

If you do break down at sea, you need to be able to call for help, so we bought two separate emergency satellite beacons, a PLB & EPIRB, from different manufacturers, each of which uses a different satellite system. We fitted a raised antenna for our VHF radio to give further coverage and rented a satellite phone.

Our good friend, paramedic and pioneer of safety at sea Peter Conroy, helped us put together a medical kit and organised specialist first-aid training for the most likely problems we might encounter. I even asked Peter about what to do in the extremely unlikely event of a shark bite to an artery – and he had an answer, haemostatic dressings, bandages with clotting agents developed by the US military. Being three to four hours from land, a cut with serious bleeding would be a major problem. You can never eliminate all risk, but you can minimise it by understanding and preparing for the likely issues and knowing how to deal with the consequences. More than anything what you need at sea is a hardy, experienced crew with what we call in Ireland 'cop on', aka common sense, and equally, to pick your weather windows wisely and patiently. That is the hardest part.

~~~~~~~

And so that was what we did, wait. Week after week, month after month. We needed a minimum four-day weather window to sail to the shelf edge, one day to get out, one day to get back and so two days out there.

From mid-June to the end of September 2016 there was no such weather window forecast west of Ireland. The charts would look promising, but then always dissipate a day or so beforehand.

I went from patient to tormented to demented, watching the ocean, trawling over forecasts and booking and cancelling and waiting again for suitable weather. Keeping all our equipment prepared and a crew on standby is no easy feat, not to mention sailing boats, spotter planes and family life. I'm fortunate to work with some unbelievably dedicated and patient people.

Kev Smith is a cameraman, drone operator, surfer and lover of all things ocean. Fortunately for me and this project, Kev lives nearby and offered fierce commitment right from the beginning. Waiting patiently for suitable shoot days, always offering considered advice and no small amount of technical acumen, Kev's contribution was enormous.

We managed one sailing trip in mid-August on a beautiful 50-foot yacht, setting sail south from Rossaveal, Co. Galway, through the Arans and towards the Blasket Islands, with hopes of reaching the Porcupine Seabight, 70 km southwest of the Blaskets. The forecast had been encouraging, if not exactly perfect, but with about 12 knots of favourable wind, we were making great headway.

South of Loop Head, Co. Clare, both wind and swell began to rise. Sadly I'm a seasick sailor, which I suppose isn't great, considering my occupation. I'm fine on RIBs, on larger boats I'm usually OK if I have a few hours to get used to the pitch and roll at sea, but to go straight into it, I find difficult.

By north Kerry, I was green and throwing up into the swell. We reached the outside of An Tíreacht, the most westerly Blasket island at 2 am, with the wind gusting 27 knots, definitely not filming weather. We ran for port in Dingle.

John Brown has been a BBC natural-history cameraman and director for 25 years, and has worked with us and been our mentor since 2008. I only wish he could work with us all the time, for if he did, our films would be beautiful beyond belief. A more creative, gifted cameraman and film-maker I doubt I'll ever meet and an absolute gentleman with it all. John agreed to sail with us, and although he spends his life trekking through jungles, swamps and plains, he wasn't enjoying this weather any more than myself.

The forecast continued to change. We went to sea again the next morning and reached Inis Mhic Aoibhleáin, the southernmost Blasket and home of Charlie Haughey for many years, but once you face the open ocean, things are very different. I did a lot of sailing when I lived in the UK, mainly in the Solent, the body of water between mainland UK and the Isle of Wight – we once even sailed from Wales to Ireland, though with little wind it was mostly motoring. Returning to Ireland, I felt experienced enough to charter a sailboat on the Atlantic coast. I will never forget the first sight of the true open Atlantic when we gave up the shelter of land. Dark green, monstrous rolling swell, coming in from the west to swallow us, we stood mouths agape.

And so this trip was becoming futile; there were humpbacks about and Kev got some drone shots, a real achievement given our state, but for filming from a boat at sea, you need fewer than 12 knots of wind and under two metres of swell. Even in his seasick state, John shot some interview pieces with Dr Joanne O'Brien, an ocean acoustics expert, and myself, and we returned in the afternoon to Dingle to drop some people off before beginning the 175 km return journey to Rossaveal. Sailing west to Slea Head and then turning north towards our 'home' port, our spirits were low.

The sight of the Blaskets, however, never ceases to raise some cheer within me. We sailed through the sound between Beginish and Dún Chaoin, north past Inis Tuaisceart, the north island, locally known as 'The Deadman' as its outline resembles a man lying with folded hands, and then on into open ocean, north towards The Loop, as seamen refer to Clare's most westerly point. The sea was still up, but the sun was painting dramatic colours through fast-moving clouds, dark greens, blues, blacks and puffy white, high oceanic cloud.

By evening we were starving, not having eaten for twelve hours, but risking time trying to cook in the galley of a rolling boat didn't appeal. You learn to watch the horizon at sea, whilst your body and mind are working out that the motion is actually OK. After a couple of days on a rolling sea, most everything is fine, then when you return to land, everything rocks again for a day or so, the drunken sailor routine, though it perhaps only explains part of that phenomenon.

Then the skipper called out and held up plates of spuds and sausages, oh my God, the nicest meal I've ever eaten, 'The food of kings,' Kev called it as we merrily slopped in the bangers and mash.

~~~~~~

About twenty kilometres west of Mutton Island, Co. Clare, just before sunset, we spotted huge flocks of diving birds – definite bait-ball activity – and then the unmistakable big, bushy blow of

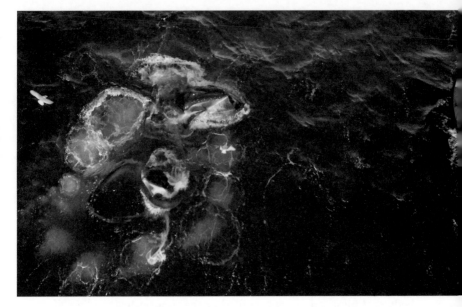

40 km west of Clare at the end of November 2016, humpbacks rising through a bubble net, with sprat leaping above the open mouth, our RIB just visible. PHOTO: KEV SMITH

a humpback whale. This was incredible. I'd been watching this area for three years now, seeing signs of this feeding, and now a whale! It was too late in the day and the sailboat just wouldn't have worked with dynamically moving bait balls, so we continued our voyage north, resolving to return to meet these animals in the next weather window.

Sadly that wouldn't come around for another six weeks, but into that October of 2016 and through November, we would have some truly amazing encounters in that very area with feeding activity, humpbacks and Minke whales, thousands of common dolphins, dozens of sea bird species and even 'shoals' of bluefin tuna. I would

Some very happy men sailing home after an amazing offshore day west of Clare. It felt like Christmas. Kev Smith, Ken, Steve Thomas and sound recordist Phillipe Faujas. PHOTO: KEV SMITH

still say my greatest experience in the natural world was on the last day of November, when, just at sunset, the sea erupted with life and marauding monsters. Seven or eight humpback whales tore up the ocean in the low sun, chasing and competing for enormous shoals of sprat, two-metre common dolphins appearing midget-like within the madness. Some humpbacks worked in pairs, blowing great rings of bubble nets underwater before rising with mouths open as wide as our boat, monsters from the deep, then other humpbacks violently lunging at the remnants of the fleeing sprat. As two humpbacks rose within five metres of our RIB, mouths agape, sprat jumping for their lives and the burning winter sun resting on the ocean behind, I thought to myself, 'This is cameraman nirvana.' It was a scene that could have been painted by the great British sea painter J. M. W. Turner in his creative obsession with the sun as a form of deity of the natural world.

~~~~~~~

And so we waited for spring. Being a small production company, we're never idle, and it's common in natural history film-making to fulfil multiple roles such as cameraman and director or producer. In Ireland shoot days are so unpredictable that this is perhaps the only way to work. In poor weather I do a producer's job, on better days I'm swimming with whales. I do most of the research, scripting and even at times editing, but perhaps, in some regards, this is a way to be a more complete film-maker, as you create the stories and follow them all the way to realisation, albeit with lots of help and work from others. Someone told me the Coen brothers edit their own films, and there are a number of feature-film directors who shoot their own films, I even heard of one American who had to use a pseudonym to avoid the union!

For my last project I worked over seven hundred days and got paid for less than half that. Once, when money was very tight, I was lying under a trailer, covered in grease, changing wheel bearings when Katrina appeared with a camera, laughing. 'Do you think the BBC lads have to do this?'

Such is life and I love it.

~~~~~~~~

The weather during the summer of 2016 was so poor that we'd had just seven shoot days on the open ocean searching for large whales. We'd managed more shoot days in November than the entire summer.

And now, summer 2017 was following the same patterns. Aside from time on *Celtic Explorer* filming the deep seabed with an ROV, we'd had just four days trying to shoot whales on the open ocean.

It takes two full days to prepare everything for a sailing trip, setting up all the camera gear, housings, dive gear, medical kits, as well as shopping for provisions and pre-cooking food so we don't have to cook dinners on board and so forth. In mid-July we saw a weather window and chartered a sailboat in West Cork, the closest land to the Porcupine Seabight, to minimise sailing time. We were in the car fully loaded after the two-day prep when my phone rang. It was the skipper. 'Have you seen the latest chart, Ken?' And so we unpacked everything and went back to spreadsheets and VAT and reading research documents. And watching weather.

By the end of August our time was almost up: we had to deliver to RTÉ who'd waited patiently, I'd even been to their season launch, a big media fanfare where I somewhat surreally found myself on stage in the midst of celebrities talking about the series – their support was immensely sustaining for us, but this was serious pressure now.

Still, we were driven to get to the shelf edge to find these animals. I sat down with the lads; Kev Smith who's been with us from the day we began, is a rock of common sense, Seamus Ó'Riain, a seasoned open-ocean yachtsman, big-wave surfer and general seafarer, and our long-time sea-faring colleague Steve Thomas. There were some possible weather windows, but they'd last no more than thirty-six hours or if we were lucky forty-eight. Could we make it to the shelf edge and back safely on the RIB? We talked, but we'd already been over it many times, we had the kit and the know-how, and at some point, we had to call it and go. This was our second year of waiting.

And so, in the last days of August, we trusted a forecast and left Dingle harbour in the early morning. The first deep-water canyons of the Porcupine Seabight are 75 km west of the outer Blaskets, themselves 25 km west of the harbourside in Dingle. It's funny how, when you wait so long for something, it can seem surreal when it happens. After driving the RIB for two hours, we were around 65 km from the mainland; for some reason I remember it was a Saturday, I suppose days appear with certain colours or even symbolism in your mind. The ocean was blue, bluer than I'd ever seen in Ireland, I felt slightly light-headed, maybe from the early start and the rocking around at sea, or just the sense of adventure.

~~~~~~~

You have to experience the vastness of the open ocean to truly understand it at an emotional level, though I guess that's true for most things in life. The Blasket Islands, even with their elevation, had long disappeared from sight and we could now only see the higher points of Mount Brandon. I was elated but worried – these men were my responsibility, and every hour we travelled from land was another hour away from safety.

Three hours from land – and although we knew from our equipment we'd reached the canyons – the sight of two large fishing trawlers left us in no doubt that we were in the right place. Their crews must have wondered what the hell we were at on our tiny boat as we waved and smiled pleasantly.

Sitting down to eat some lunch, the mandatory Irishman's fare of spuds and butter, I'd hardly swallowed a mouthful when we heard the sweet sound that is a whale blow, followed by another and then another. Long-finned pilot whales, one after another, I'd never been so close: the bigger ones appeared jet black, and calves rose close by adults, though there were all sizes of animals, perhaps thirty or forty in the group. They swam north past us, then back around in a wide circle. This was my chance and with bits of spud still between my teeth, I was biting on a snorkel and swimming into their line of travel. I've done all the thinking, sometimes too much thinking, six years of it, this was it. I'd never been in blue water before in Ireland, this was the open ocean with no run-off from land to cloud the sea and paint the water green.

A lead group of four pilot whales, all different sizes, approach. I gently fin close into their path and notice their eyes fixed on me as their bodies ease forward; there's a small calf still with neonatal skin folds from its time in its mother's womb, she was likely the eight-metre animal in the middle of the group … just as she approaches, she jerks her head towards me and my heart jumps in

Long-finned pilot whales on the Porcupine Seabight

my chest, but she turns away as if in signal to the younger ones to keep going, and in a moment I watch them disappear into the dark blue water, like a fleeting dream you struggle to recall on waking … but the feeling stays.

Back on the RIB, the entire pod of pilot whales tracks alongside us as we venture along the canyon that runs south-west for another 10 km. They rise from the ocean, the adults with deep, baritone blows, and the calves with light, childlike breaths, all of them swimming alongside as if patrolling the deep ocean on behalf of some greater entity or even deity. Sometimes as they rise out through the swell, their bulbous heads emerge in full for a moment, their eyes clearly observing the strange sight of us.

There are lots of sea birds, tiny and astonishing storm petrels just 15 cm long but not looking too worried about being 110 km

*Gannets diving for mackerel in a deep-water canyon near the
Porcupine Seabight*

offshore, gulls, gannets and the odd great skua, a predatory bird,
patrolling and swooping. We'd seen almost no life all the way from
the Blaskets up to the shelf edge, but here is an oasis of life in
the open ocean, this was what I'd dreamed of and hoped for, for
six years.

We drift easily along the canyon, a small number of gannets
diving and emerging from the deep blue water with mackerel,
struggling hopelessly now in the last moments of their short lives,
sides of flashing blue, turquoise and even shimmers of gold, bowing
in farewell to the sun God.

I thought I saw bottlenose dolphins in the distance, a great
opportunity for offshore photo identification, but the weather was
changing and I had pangs of fear at the thought of big seas. It
might seem obvious now, but when you're on land reading sea

forecasts, you're usually looking at the coast, and one of things we'd realised was that we needed calm seas for the entire area out and back. Sea conditions can vary greatly over even short distances of maybe twenty kilometres, you can sometimes even see different weather systems from the panoramic view the open ocean affords you.

I once had the privilege of spending a couple of days on Skelligs Rock with Aidan Walsh, the lighthouse keeper there for many years, and now sadly departed from us, all too young. The weather was turning and we were advised to get off the rock onto the next boat. Watching the skies, Aidan raised his arm, pointing north; there was a long blue gap in the cloud, beyond which sat very different, dispersed cloud formations. 'Look, there's a break in the weather systems, you'll be OK back in Clare,' Aidan told me gently and sure enough his word was good.

After just three hours on the shelf edge, we turn the RIB for home, a little nervous but elated from our experiences. Sure enough the sky darkens, swell rises and progress is much slower. After a couple of hours I give Seamus a break and drive for a while; the raindrops are now so piercing that I can hardly keep my eyes open so I put on my dive mask, which looks somewhat absurd. It takes three and a half hours to reach Inis Mhic Aoibhleáin from the shelf edge, I was never so glad to see that beautiful rock, we drive between there and Inis na Bró and I'm tempted to test the legend that the Haugheys never refuse hostelry to sailors, but we carry on. An hour later, we climb onto the harbourside in Dingle, my ageing back creaking. It had taken four and a half hours to make our port.

~~~~~~

The Azores High is a weather system usually hovering over those islands and the sub-tropics, but it will occasionally push north into our latitudes, and as August turned to September, it had obliged, and we could see a weather window west of Mayo. Our confidence was high and after barely a couple of nights at home we hauled the RIB to the westernmost part of Mayo, a five-and-a-half-hour drive. Kev had gone ahead and found a great slipway to launch from, and just after sunrise we went to sea. At 65 km, this is the closest land in Ireland to the edge of the continental shelf. The seabed drops down into the Rockall Trough; in places the depth falls away from 200 to 3,000 metres, within just a two-kilometre lateral distance. If you think that Mount Everest summit is a similar height of 3,000 metres above base camp, but with a lateral distance of about 15 km, you get a sense of the sheerness of the drop-off of the shelf edge.

Just as our equipment told us we were crossing the edge, with the depth gauge reading 900 m, an enormous whale rises and blows; I only get a glimpse and thought it had a blueish tinge. My God, a blue whale, could it be? All is quiet for ten minutes, then an animal rises and blows again, within forty metres of the RIB, tracking alongside us – a fin whale, the second-largest animal ever, growing up to twenty-four metres. Whether the first animal was a blue we'll never know, but I slip into the gin-clear blue water, oh my God, it was even clearer than on the Porcupine, you could see for thirty metres; I've never witnessed anything like this in

Tracking alongside a fin whale over the Rockall Basin. PHOTO: KEV SMITH

Ireland. The fin whale makes one fleeting, heart-stopping pass in the water, but Kev gets some incredible drone footage. It's more than twice the length of our eight-metre RIB.

We carry on and in no time hear the familiar soft blow of pilot whales, about twenty of them, in fact. The sun shines down on these tropical-looking waters, I put on short bodyboard fins to kick up less water in the glassy sea and gently fin into the animals' path. At first they turned away, but then a group of about eight

swim around and literally within a metre of me, there's a small calf in the middle and other animals appear to change position to come between me and the calf. I stay as still as I can in the water and watch this magical scene. The whales swim around, back and forth for perhaps twenty minutes – refracted through

FOLLOWING SPREAD: *Pod of long-finned pilot whales diving in 3,000 metres of water over the Rockall Basin, west of Mayo*

seawater, the sun's rays split into a thousand shards, each catching and illuminating the animals' seasoned and battle-scarred skin. They seem to move as almost a single entity, anticipating each other's changes of direction, and then they dive, slowly and almost dreamily, for the deep. I'm sad to see them leave for I know this was likely a once-in-a-lifetime opportunity, but there is something beautiful, poignant even, about the brevity of the experience.

Pilot whales live in matrilineal groups, meaning both males and females remain with their mother for most of their lives; this behaviour is probably the origin of their name, as groups follow a single leader. Sadly, it also explains why large groups sometimes appear in shallow coastal waters, even stranding and dying, perhaps as they follow a sick, older animal. There have been many such tragedies, with one on Rutland Island off the coast of Donegal in 2010 where thirty-three animals died.

We carry on across the edge, and after an hour or so encounter another fin whale; it moves quickly and elusively, we don't chase it. Then an animal about six metres long rises and blows: it has a creamy brown, heavily scarred body with a slightly bulging forehead. I get a reasonable photograph and I believe it to have been the extremely rare Cuvier's beaked whale, the deepest-diving of all whales with a recorded dive of almost 3,000 metres over two hours. And we think five-minute breath holds are an achievement!

~~~~~~~

The following day we make the same journey, but this time the coastal waters are severely windy and rough; we tough it out for an hour and eventually reach glassy calm waters, which we have for the remainder of the day. Our holy grails, if there can be a plural, are blue and sperm whales. There are just four or five photos of blues in Irish waters and, as far as I know, just a single blurry image of a sperm whale. We'd drafted in a spotter plane, which flew up from Cork with two cetacean experts, Róisín Pinfield and Mick Mackey. From sea level you see so very little, so the plane flew transects of about twenty kilometres at a time back and forth over the five canyons beneath us. I got a bit emotional when the plane came into sight at first, almost like, we've worked so hard to do this, and now someone is out here helping us ...

We chat with Mick over the radio; they've flown over all the canyons but seen no large whales. I asked them to try another pass, at which point fuel constraints would necessitate their return to Cork.

Less than an hour later I hear Róisín's voice on the radio, but it's very broken: 'We ... *khhhhhhh* ... a sperm whale ...'. We call and call but she can't hear us and we only receive back the odd word from her. They're out of coverage and our radio range doesn't extend that far into the air. We have no idea where the plane is at that point, they could be in any direction. I call to Róisín to fly towards where they'd last seen us and vainly hope she'll hear. I could have cried, years of work to get here and to have come so close and then miss out. We rack our brains, feeling helpless on our tiny boat in this vast ocean.

Fifteen minutes pass and then Róisín's voice comes over the radio loud and clear and in a no-nonsense fashion: 'Ten degrees five one, point seven seven four.' We drive the twenty kilometres to where they had seen and photographed two sperm whales, but the journey takes half an hour and we arrive to an empty sea.

Sperm whales can dive for anything from thirty to ninety minutes, so we wait and wait. Kev puts up the drone and flies back and forth searching a vast area, and although the sea remained glassy, there are no signs of any whales or dolphins. I put a hydrophone into the water and am stunned by the amount of cetacean sounds. There are clear whistles and clicks, back and forth, almost as if the animals are answering one another. I hear a continuous loud click that I suspect is a sperm whale hunting. They use echolocation in the darkness of the deep to find their prey, usually octopus and squid and often the elusive giant squid, whose tentacles are estimated to be up to thirty metres wide, a creature from a Jules Verne adventure. We do some interview pieces, with me bursting with excitement and relief at having made it to the shelf edge after years of trying. With just the three of us there and Kev shooting, Seamus steps in as sound recordist, with the boom pole and microphone, a true multitasker – he did a sterling job.

If you've ever held a microphone, you'll recognise the kind of 'thud' sounds you get when touching the sensitive bit of the mic off anything. I was hearing this through the hydrophone and couldn't understand what it was. I'd used a 50-metre cable to submerge the hydrophone as far as possible away from the sounds of the water

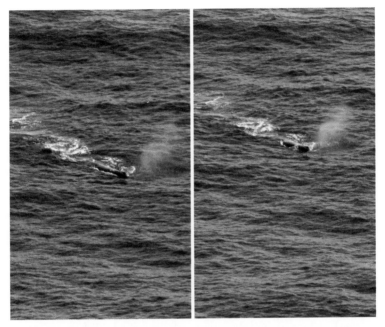

Sperm whales photographed by Mick Mackey from our spotter plane over the Rockall Trough

surface, but the mic was omnidirectional and I wondered if it was picking up the sound of the RIB slapping on the water.

After waiting another hour or so we turn for home, disappointed but still relieved at what we'd managed to document. It was a Friday evening, the first day of September, and we couldn't get over the number of aircraft overhead, dozens and dozens, at times their moisture trails seeming to cover half the sky – I guess weekend trippers to New York.

We made it back to land in under two hours on the flat, calm sea. A great sense of relief came over us, particularly Kev and myself who had soldiered on now for two years to accomplish this, although he remained professional to the end, insisting we get drone shots of towing the RIB along the Mullet Peninsula. Although we didn't know it then, it would be a whole winter before we went to sea again. On the long drive back to Clare with Seamus, we stopped at a railroad crossing, Aretha Franklin's 'Say a Little Prayer' came over the radio, I closed my eyes and thought I'd never been happier.

~~~~~~~

Later Dr Joanne O'Brien confirmed that the clicks we recorded were indeed those of sperm whales hunting and likely the two animals Mick and Róisín had photographed from our spotter plane. But Joanne had dark news: the thud, which I thought was the RIB on the sea, was actually the sound of seismic surveying, air guns blasting down to the seabed from a ship to check whether the geological profile indicated suitability or likelihood of buried oil and gas reserves.

We looked at records for seismic activity in the relevant government departments and I was shocked to discover that the nearest activity on that day was 400 km to the south on the Porcupine Bank. If this was loud to my human ears from 400 km away, how did it sound to animals close by, whose primary sense was hearing?

You may ask why all this effort is important or even justifiable. Well in over two years' work, we managed to document eight different species of whales – six in Irish waters – and some of their behaviour for the first time ever. We documented basking shark courtship behaviour for the first time anywhere in the world and made long-distance matches of the critically endangered blue whale between Iceland and the Azores, the first ever three-way match in the eastern North Atlantic. Using a photo of a blue taken by Mick Baines and Maren Reichelt in Ireland and working with research scientists in Canada, Iceland, Denmark, the Azores and Ireland, we matched that animal to the Azores, meaning this was clear-cut evidence of the spring northward migration route of blue whales from the tropics to Icelandic and Arctic waters as well as the autumnal southward migration back towards the tropics and past Ireland.

Six scientific research papers are being written about these various subjects, an unprecedented number for a TV documentary, and I am proud to the point of being emotional that sixteen sections from *Ireland's DEEP ATLANTIC* are now included in the Junior Cycle school curriculum in Ireland, meaning that every Irish teenager will now experience the amazing creatures and habitats of our rich ocean world. But they will also learn about conservation and environmental issues, such as the impact of consumer spending habits on the ocean and the planet, and the consequences of plastic and sound pollution in the ocean.

Education, awareness and an emotional response to the natural world are what will, I hope, help to turn around our destruction of the planet we share with billions of other creatures. I know I've done my best to help. That is all any of us can do.

Ireland's DEEP ATLANTIC was broadcast by RTÉ in April 2018 to a rapturous response from the Irish public. I genuinely wasn't prepared for the avalanche of positive coverage and particularly social media commentary, much of it highly emotional and praiseworthy.

One particular tweet does stand out:

@Ruairi #Irelandsdeepatlantic is blowing my fucking mind! By far the best natural history programme about Ireland I've ever seen. Worth my whole years licence fee! #RTE

THE PLANET

*For those who could not hear the music, the dancers
appeared as lunatics.*

HUMANS HAVE EXISTED, at least in their current form of *Homo
sapiens*, for somewhere between 200,000 and 300,000 years. Prior
to this, we can trace our evolutionary lineage through stages of
various primate species going back tens of millions of years.

For almost all of that time period, humans (and all our
evolutionary predecessors) have lived within the natural world,
within or close to forests, plains, riverbanks, mountains and ocean
coasts. That also means close to trees, plants, wild animals, birds,
insects and, of course, the weather.

Although there were ancient city-dwelling civilisations in
parts of the world, I think it's fair to say that the vast majority
lived very close to nature until perhaps one hundred years ago.
Globally, most of us now live in urban areas and work in offices and
factories. Such change in such a short period, has been dramatic
for us to cope with. All of our primal senses and instincts were
developed in inordinately different surroundings. Is it any wonder
then, that we go to nature when in need of rest, restitution or to
deal with emotional issues?

But change will always be a part of the world.

In a few hundred thousand years after humans have disappeared from Earth, the planet will have returned to how it once was. More or less.

Life persists, and once our influence has faded, forests will regrow, animals now on the brink of extinction may even recover, ice ages will come and go and sea levels will fall and rise, though new species will begin to ascend and dominate because life on Earth has never stayed the same for two consecutive seconds. Evolution is the nature of the universe.

There will be more mass extinctions, just as happened with dinosaurs and later humans, though we can't hold dinosaurs to account for the asteroid which finished their existence – unlike the reasons why human life will decline. There will be continual evolution and adaptation among species of life. Primates, if they are still around, may even evolve into some human-like form, and if that does occur, I would truly love to know whether the same mistakes will be made – or perhaps I wouldn't.

I wonder whether Carl Linnaeus had a wicked sense of humour. He was the genius Swedish zoologist who in the 1700s developed the formal naming system for all forms of life whereby two Latin names are used for every species, such as *Homo erectus*. The first part is the genus, the group to which something belongs, and the second part is something specific to the species. For example, fin whales are known as *Balaenoptera physalus*, *Balaenoptera* meaning winged or finned whale and *physalus* meaning blowpipe or blowhole, referring to the animals' enormous nostrils, which emit enormous breath blows.

Peculiarly, Linnaeus named blue whales *Balaenoptera musculus*, which people take to mean 'muscular finned whale' but actually means 'little mouse-finned whale'. And so, perhaps in a similar manner, Linnaeus defined human beings as *Homo sapiens* meaning 'wise man' in Latin.

I say the world will more or less return to pre-*Homo sapiens* form, but this isn't quite true because many of the changes introduced by us will prevent things reverting to how they were before our time. For example, the decimation and confusion prevalent within many ecosystems will struggle to unravel: plants or animals brought from one part of the world to another and becoming alien species within their new habitat have frequently thrived and dominated and will continue to do so at the expense of native species, some of which have become extinct and won't return. For example, rhododendron is a beautiful-looking plant which somehow made it to Ireland, and in the 19th century began colonising areas such as the ancient oak forests of Killarney's national park. Rhododendron grows so thickly that it out-competes native flora, including crucially, small oak saplings. The sad reality is that this ancient native forest is now a living ghost, for there are no new trees to take over from the great oaks.

We see this same pattern in the sea. *Sargassum muticum* is an invasive species of seaweed first seen in Ireland in the early 1970s. Nicknamed wireweed, it grows so thick that by early summer it's almost impossible to swim through, and I've found myself almost trapped in its vast 'underwater forests'. This prevents growth of native seaweeds and blocks light making it to the seabed, which then diminishes growth of a multitude of native creatures and plants.

When humans have gone, what will be the fate of the billions of domesticated animals in the world should they survive the worst effects of global warming, habitat destruction and species loss? What will all the cows, chickens, sheep, pigs, dogs, cats and hamsters do when we're gone? And then there are our weapons and nuclear technologies. Whilst I'm no expert on these, I do understand that the unexploded nuclear power harnessed across the world could in all likelihood destroy the planet, and it's hard to see us disarming all of that on our 'way out the door'.

I write this in resignation and defeat. I spend my life trying to document the natural world and create awareness and education. When I'm feeling particularly despondent I tell myself, just do as much as you can, that's all that's possible. I intend never to give up trying to document the natural world and to raise awareness of the environmental and conservation issues we have created. I'll never give up telling stories from the ocean of empty reefs, of ecosystems chronically out of balance because of overfishing, of the pervasive issue of plastics in the ocean, even on coral reefs 2,000 metres deep, of damage to coastal waters from nitrate run-off, of dead dolphins and whales needlessly killed by human activities, of the impact of sound pollution in the ocean ... the list seems endless.

But let's keep some balance too. Despite all of this, the seas around Ireland are not in terminal decline; our oceans are vast, and nature is incredibly robust and fights endlessly to survive. Plants, animals and habitats can recover if you can leave them alone for long enough.

But overall, we're losing the battle. As much as I hate to admit it, no rational person would bet that we're going to change our ways in time to address climate change and prevent potential chaos and destruction.

~~~~~~

I remember the early 1990s TV documentaries about the destruction of the Amazon rainforests, swathes of ancient, beautiful forests being cut down for timber; the same forests that create so much of the oxygen breathed by every life form on Earth.

A global outcry ensued. Sting, frontman for The Police and one of the biggest rock stars in the world at the time, joined an Amazonian tribal leader. Hand in hand they would tackle the government, the loggers, the loss of flora and fauna, and displaced peoples, some of whom had lived in isolation from the rest of humanity almost since the beginning. The world was standing up to this problem and we would address it – we were filled with hope.

Almost thirty years later we're told that across the world, forest areas the size of Italy – 30 million hectares – are cut down every year. Tree loss worldwide has doubled since 2004, while deforestation of crucial tropical rainforests has doubled since 2008. These vast areas continue to be cleared for soy, beef, palm oil, timber and other globally traded commodities – commodities we consume every day.

Trees not only absorb vast quantities of the carbon emitted in the world, so helping to curb climate change, they also emit huge amounts of carbon when cut down – a double whammy with the loss of every tree.

Until the 1600s vast areas of Ireland were covered by forests especially ancient oak trees. It's estimated that the great majority of these were cut down within a hundred years, largely to build the British navy but also to rebuild London after the Great Fire of 1666. I've read that the British introduced a law at that time prohibiting the building of wooden houses in Dublin so as to make Irish timber available to build houses in Britain.

A 2019 United Nations study estimates that up to one million plant and animal species face extinction within decades due to human activities. One million. Without immediate action to conserve habitats, the rate of species extinction, which is already tens to hundreds of times higher than the average across the past ten million years, will only increase. The report states that agriculture has had the biggest impact on those ecosystems people depend on for food, clean water and a stable climate, and that, startlingly, the loss of species and habitats poses as much a danger to life on Earth as does climate change. An October 2018 report from the World Wildlife Fund states that humanity has wiped out a staggering 60 per cent of animal populations since 1970.

But we already know this.

~~~~~~

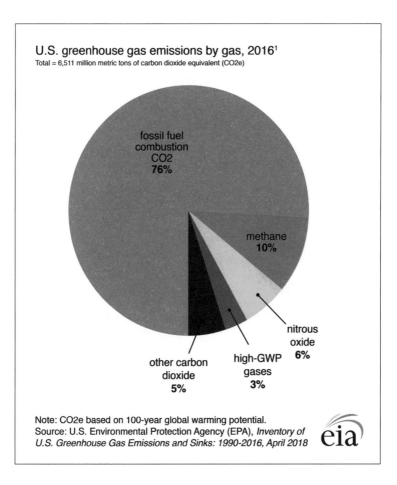

U.S. greenhouse gas emissions by gas, 2016[1]
Total = 6,511 million metric tons of carbon dioxide equivalent (CO2e)

fossil fuel
combustion
CO2
76%

methane
10%

nitrous
oxide
6%

high-GWP
gases
3%

other carbon
dioxide
5%

Note: CO2e based on 100-year global warming potential.
Source: U.S. Environmental Protection Agency (EPA), *Inventory of
U.S. Greenhouse Gas Emissions and Sinks: 1990-2016, April 2018*

eia

Recently someone said to me, 'Ken, farming is a thirteen-billion-euro industry in Ireland – you can't be giving out about that!' I didn't respond, I couldn't.

Planet Earth's climate is warming largely due to greenhouse gases generated by human activities. These gases rise up into the atmosphere where they lodge and trap heat just like the roof of a greenhouse or polytunnel. Carbon dioxide forms the largest of the greenhouse gases and is emitted during the burning of fossil fuels,

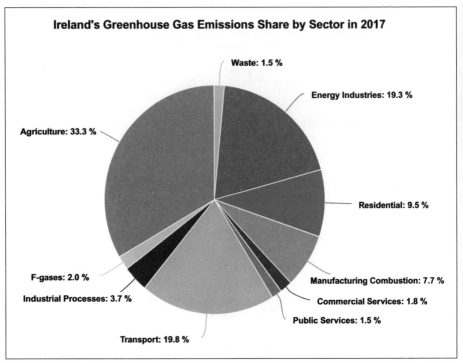

Ireland's Greenhouse Gas Emissions Share by Sector in 2017

Waste: 1.5 %

Energy Industries: 19.3 %

Agriculture: 33.3 %

Residential: 9.5 %

F-gases: 2.0 %

Industrial Processes: 3.7 %

Manufacturing Combustion: 7.7 %

Commercial Services: 1.8 %

Public Services: 1.5 %

Transport: 19.8 %

SOURCE: EPA IRELAND 2019

petrol, diesel, coal, gas and turf as well as, of course, when tress are cut down and bogs cut. There are also natural sources of CO_2, which comprise a smaller portion of the total.

Sources of greenhouse gas (GHG) emissions differ across countries, depending on local industry, climate, transport etc. Refrigeration is one of the biggest global consumers of energy, as is transport; and not forgetting domestic and freight exhaust emissions, the vans and trucks that bring consumer goods to our door, much of which is also shipped by sea. Shipping has risen hugely in recent years with the global surge in consumer buying, especially from China to the rest of the world. And of course there's air travel, carrying both cargo and people. Although newer aircraft are far more efficient in terms of fuel usage, the numbers of people globally using air travel is on a significant trajectory: figures predict a 250 to 300 per cent rise in tourist numbers globally in the next 10 to 15 years, which seems to match predictions for new long-haul aircraft manufacture – but folks in industry worth billions of dollars tend to do their homework.

Electricity and heat generation form another huge part of GHG emission sources, heating our homes and workplaces, many of which lack proper insulation. Computer data centres, which form the infrastructure of the internet and companies' own computing infrastructures, consume vast amounts of energy. Every time we browse the web or send an email, energy is burned – billions of people use the internet and communicate with each other 24/7 across local Wi-Fi routers and mobile-phone masts all the way to a data centre in India or China or Ireland. Think of the energy used every time we charge our phone or keep our laptops plugged in.

~~~~~~

While most of the above sources emit carbon dioxide, the other significant greenhouse gases are methane, nitrous oxide and fluoride gases. Methane has up to twenty-five times more impact as a greenhouse gas than carbon dioxide and has several 'natural' sources such as wetlands, but in Ireland, 85 per cent of methane is produced by agriculture, with methane itself accounting for the largest portion of agricultural greenhouse gases. Cattle and sheep release methane as a by-product of microbial fermentation of food in the rumen and large intestine. This process, called enteric fermentation, produces more than half of all GHG emissions from agriculture. In addition, nitrous oxide is released when nitrogen fertiliser is spread on grasslands.

~~~~~~

Farming is very close to our hearts in Ireland; land cultivation and animal husbandry have been carried out for almost as long as people have been here. Up until the early 1970s, the majority of Irish people were either farmers or lived in villages or small towns close to the land and the countryside. Rural living is a core part of who we are in Ireland; it is our connection to nature, to landscape and to our ancient rural culture, which has sustained us for thousands of years. It was the great poet and philosopher John Moriarty who said that 'Our culture is what shelters us from the cold blast of meaninglessness.' Wow.

Spending time in the natural world is crucial to our emotional and physical well-being. The legendary Irish warrior / hunter, Fionn Mac Cumhail is reputed to have coined the phrase the 'music of what happens' in the context of finding yourself in nature. Again and again research shows the importance of nature in our lives. For example, children who live near park areas in cities are more balanced and developed than those who don't. Adults in these areas suffer less stress and anxiety and consequently have better physical and mental health.

For people from my father's time, living on an island farm, the weather and the seasons meant everything to them in how they lived and ate and how they worked and undoubtedly how they felt. In spring they sowed crops of potatoes, carrots and turnips for their own consumption, and sugar beet to sell commercially. In late summer they cut and saved hay for winter feed for their dairy cows and horses and in early autumn they harvested their other crops.

~~~~~~~

In 2019 farmers were cutting silage in January, and as I write in mid-May, many farmers are again cutting silage, some from the same fields. The cliffs that I walked as a child have, in some places, eroded as much as five metres, but much of that was from just two winters of storms between 2013 and 2015. The old people say they have never known the ferocity and frequency of the storms we've had in recent winters. Weather has never, in the history of the planet, been even and consistent, that's the nature of nature, if you like, but our climate has already changed and warmed, and that of course causes a chain of events, because in the natural world, everything is connected.

I live in a rural area surrounded by small farmers; my uncles were dairy farmers for decades, my wife grew up on a farm and her brother is still a dairy farmer. I understand the challenges of trying make a living from farming. In fact, having grown up in a family of eight children, having been an immigrant for thirteen years, having swept streets and dug holes for a living in sub-zero temperatures as an illegal immigrant, having been broke and then successful and then broke again as a film-maker, I understand as much as any man can the challenges of making a living.

Farming has changed so dramatically as to be almost unrecognisable from fifty years ago. Farming, you see, like most all other consumer-related production, suffers from a relentless pressure to drive prices lower for the end consumer and of course, the benefit of the businesses which trade this produce between the producer and the consumer.

Forty years ago, my uncles had around twenty-five dairy cows and made a reasonable living from that. I believe farmers received the equivalent of about 15 cent per litre for their milk, while in the shops people paid circa 29 cent per litre.

Forty years later and while contracts differ, I know some farmers now receive about 30 cent per litre and the average price to the consumer is between €1.10 and €1.25. In that time the quality of milk being produced has dramatically increased with available science and technology.

According to the consumer price index, something which cost 15 cent in 1979 would now cost 67 cent and the same milk for which consumers paid 29 cent should now cost €1.11, which it does. So accounting for inflation, the price now paid to farmers is less than half what it was forty years ago. EU grants may compensate partially for this, but realistically won't be available for ever.

I find it odd that we're happy to pay €2.50 for a litre of water, but expect to buy milk for just €1.10. Imagine the difference an extra 5 or 10 cent a litre would make to famers' ability to earn a living and farm in an ecologically sustainable way. Of course a lot of milk is used in other dairy-based products such as cheese or powdered milk, but the portion of the retail price of these products paid to the producer is still relatively small.

Farmers, therefore, like all consumer-related industries must go for economies of scale so as to survive: high volume–low margin. In Ireland many farmers have doubled the size of their dairy and beef herds in recent years, putting huge additional pressure on themselves by milking twice as many cows twice a day, or feeding beef cattle and placing consequent pressure on the lands they graze, the areas where nitrogen fertilisers are spread on grass, and causing nitrate run-off into our rivers, lakes and seas – which in itself releases nitrous oxide, a greenhouse gas, into the air. Then there's all the additional slurry a herd twice the previous size generates, huge amounts of which are then spread as fertiliser due to the nitrogen, phosphorous and potassium content but which can subsequently cause nitrate run-off. Slurry also contains high levels of ammonia and pathogens such as E.coli and cryptosporidium, I have been sick many times from swallowing seawater in areas with agricultural runoff. And then there's the animal welfare issue, which I guess is an ideological matter for people to decide on.

But then most folks are removed from these issues. I was flabbergasted to discover that about 25 per cent of potatoes and carrots are thrown away before they reach supermarkets because they're too ugly. It's true. Consumer surveys show that people don't like odd-shaped vegetables, so producers either throw away 25 per cent of their produce or feed it to animals, despite all the energy it has taken to grow these. Me, I love spuds and carrots that are twisted and covered in mud, my instinctual self tells me that this means they're real and natural.

Food waste in Ireland and indeed across the western world has grown significantly: think of how much food goes into our bins, uneaten food from our plates or past its expiry, think of all the uneaten food in restaurants, I once worked as a busboy (the guy who cleans the plates and food from the tables) in a restaurant in America and was shocked at the volume of food thrown away. I reckon up to 30 per cent of food served wasn't eaten and so dumped. Think of all the energy it's taken to produce such wasted food.

———

When people talk about 'the environment' I try not to despair. It's a poor word. The environment feels like something distant, almost semi-imagined; perhaps we should just call it 'the world'. It's the place where we live, it's every place and every natural thing all around us – maybe if we think of it in this slightly different context, it may mean more to us. We could call ourselves 'worldists'.

I have to believe that if we become aware of serious issues, and understand them in an emotional sense, largely, most people will do something to help, if they can.

It's sad that in the past some environmentalists went about their work in a way that wasn't entirely helpful, perhaps pointing fingers and not actually working with communities, officials or politicians, maybe overstating their cases, which will always damage credibility. But then, broadly speaking, most environmentalists that I'm aware of were largely correct in their assessments of environmental – or let's call them 'world' – issues.

And of course the same is true for the 'other side'. People who dismiss environmentalists as tree-huggers delaying the building of a new motorway over snails, people who care more about the environment than the world, as though the two were separate things, that kind of polarised, even populist, dismissive thinking. There's a well-known story of a former government minister who, on being informed in an open meeting that there was an objection by a state department concerned with heritage to his plans for a development project, turned to his sidekick and loudly bleated: 'I thought we got rid of those fuckers?'

Debate is the hard-won luxury of democracy, and consensus a consequent symptom of civilisation.

In 2018 United Nations scientists warned that if we could keep the rise in GHG emissions at or below a level which caused the global climate to rise by 1.5 degrees compared to the mid-nineteenth-century pre-industrial revolution levels, we stood a chance of curtailing some of the worst impact of climate change.

But current trends are headed towards a rise of 3 degrees, which is predicted to have a devastating impact.

In Ireland, we are committed to a legally-binding EU target of reducing GHG emissions by 20 per cent (on 2005 levels) before 2020. The latest figures available show that with just over a year to that date, we have only reduced these by 1 per cent and so Ireland now faces EU fines of potentially hundreds of millions of euro on top of not addressing the problem and the consequent damage to the world.

~~~~~~

In one of his rare interviews, I heard Van Morrison talk about there being a 'change of consciousness' in the world in the late 1960s, specifically 1968. Sadly, he said, it didn't last and somehow closed off again by 1970. Although the Berkeley and other US student movements had already begun, 1968 was a seminal year with protests for civil rights, freedom of speech and opposition to the Vietnam War gathering huge momentum and power in the US. May 1968 saw the Paris student riots, a turning point in French and wider European social history where students and later workers spontaneously occupied universities and factories, demanding inherent social change from the ruling political classes. That same year also saw the civil rights marches begin in Northern Ireland, where Catholics took to the streets to challenge inequality and discrimination.

And look at the music from the last years of the decade, The Beatles' *Sgt. Pepper's Lonely Hearts Club Band* and *Abbey Road*,

Marvin Gaye's *I Heard It Through the Grapevine*, classic albums from the likes of Jimi Hendrix, The Rolling Stones, David Bowie, Creedence Clearwater Revival, The Doors, Cream, The Jackson 5, Procol Harum, The Who, The Moody Blues, Led Zeppelin, while the likes of Aretha Franklin, Jackie Wilson, Smokey Robinson and even Frank Sinatra were still producing classics. In Van's case perhaps two of his best ever albums, *Astral Weeks* and *Moondance* came in these few short years, while of course 1969 was the year of Woodstock, the grand-daddy of all rock festivals.

I don't encourage revolution or civil disorder as a way to achieve goals or social change in our current world. Unlike in 1968, everyone now has access to some form of media channel to make their feelings known, albeit in a very crowded space, but issues that are truly important to the world such as climate change or biodiversity loss (or to give it a simpler name, destruction of animals and the places where they live) can be publicised and discussed. People can make change; politicians follow public opinion if it's strong enough.

It's easy to complain about stuff, you may even feel as though you're doing something by having a moan, but it's an awful lot harder to get up and do something about real issues; yet we can do this. The notion of blame, be it on the government, the council, civil servants and so forth is to a large degree an attempt to transfer responsibility. If you have a problem with single-use plastics in supermarkets, write to the CEO of your supermarket. If you feel politicians aren't doing enough about climate change, write to them, write to newspapers, organise people to make their voices heard. You have to work with people to achieve real change, collaborate and encourage, create awareness of the issues. The idea of how the world should be versus how it is, is our eternal quandary, but everyone can and must do something to help slow down climate change.

I'm reminded of a man whose sixteen-year-old daughter recently asked for a lift to the city to attend a climate change protest march. 'Could you cycle?' he asked.

~~~~~~~

But you know, perhaps Carl Linnaeus was right. We are an incredibly clever, sophisticated species. Think of all our technologies, medical advances, interplanetary transport, of the thousands of languages with all their nuances that humans use to speak to each other, our music, our ability to empathise with one another ... our achievements are endless. You know, we are an incredible species, and maybe the acknowledgement of all of these achievements and abilities has been missing from the narrative on climate change and species destruction. We don't need to wipe out farming or fishing or transport or our modern way of living, we just need to change how we do things, and in some cases not even all that much. More browbeating about how and why our way of life is bringing on planetary self-destruction hasn't helped, so maybe a different approach is needed.

We may have listened, but we haven't absorbed the news. We haven't heard the music.

WHERE WE
COME FROM

I SPENT THIRTEEN YEARS away from Ireland, including four
summers and almost three years in America. Recently I hear
the word 'expat' used to describe people living away from their
home country. We used to be known as immigrants, and I recall
one Christmas landing in Shannon airport to be greeted by a
huge neon sign flashing *WELCOME HOME IMMIGRANTS*.
I suppose the sentiment was good.

The more years I spent away from home, the more my mind
would drift back to my youth, to happy and sad places, people
I loved and people I didn't, pillars in my formation as a person.
Whenever I got drunk in The Bronx, or Queens or North London,
the places where I spent my twenties, my mind would drift back to
my youth, and to summers and the old folks, my colourful aunts
and uncles and their stories and life stories and inevitably to days
and weeks lost by the sea. Dry sandy eyes from rising at 4 am to go
fishing on Fenit Island, sore fingers from pulling dogfish and crabs
out of nets, and the rich salty air, so full of lore and drenched in
the stories of my people …

'Long Jack' my great-uncle who, legend claims, when ploughing
adjacent fields, rather than walk the plough and its two horses to
the far end to traverse the gate, would instead loosen the horses,

give them a slap and lift the plough over the four-foot wall. Or the night my grandfather gave the order to cut loose the haul net when the canoe was being towed by 'something dastardly' into the deadly tidal channel at Oiléain na Choise. My father couldn't comprehend the decision to lose such a valuable family asset, but my grandfather knew better. I wandered through the fields and along the tidal shore, where every little corner and patch had a story or a name, and I met the happy ghosts of these places every time I passed or thought of them from the distance of decades and thousands of miles. This place felt like mine, and I it.

They held the art of conversation, the old folk, always knowing when to say something, and more impactfully, when not to. I felt like a newborn foal, stumbling over, trying to speak with them. For their language was that of twenty generations, of learned nuances and stories and reading people, knowing in the most sympathetic of senses, the mood or intent of another person. 'Ah he's grand, your man, as long as you go with him,' they say in reference to some cranky fecker, at once defining the man's unreasonableness and implied insecurity – a modern-day counsellor might take ten minutes to not even achieve the same clarity. I guess much of it is down to time, taking time to reflect and ponder, and finding solid ground before delivering thoughts and opinions. And knowing who you are.

And oh could they recite poetry, verse after musical verse; I wondered which they learnt first, poetry or conversation? The legendary Uileann piper Willie Clancy once said that to play traditional music one had to speak traditional language, I humbly agree – the sounds we hear and the utterances we make are intertwined and bound to the nuances of our place. It's almost impossible for a person to truly fake the accent of another locality. During World War Two Dutch resistance fighters would interrogate suspected German infiltrators by asking them to pronounce the name of the seaside town, Scheveningen: only a Dutch person could say it correctly, 'sshcley-fing-eing-gennn'. To hear a Welsh person say Llanelli, '*Chhhlanettleee*', not just the sound, but the innocence in their pronunciation – such is the notion of a sense of community or place, of a uniqueness, however marginally different from other places. This forms our sense of identity.

My American and English cousins would regard themselves as Irish, almost as much as the nationality of their birth countries. They've told us much about our family's history that we never knew: it's a recurring story of the immigrant retaining, perhaps even clinging, to their cultural identity. With successive generations, this can create a somewhat confused sense of identity and self. The Smiths' Morrissey, son of Irish immigrants to Britain, wrote extensively of this, of being regarded as Irish when in England and English by his Irish cousins. Morrissey's lyrics are now on some college syllabuses in California where US-born people of South American extraction grapple with the same issues of cultural identity.

~~~~~~~

My Irish language skills aren't good enough to truly understand Aran Island poet Mairtín Ó'Direaín's seminal poem 'Stoite', but I understand enough to know it's about a sense of place, and displacement, *'in achrann leis an saol / ag coraíocht leis an gcarraig loim'* – 'grappling with life / wrestling with grey rock'. Like so many islanders, Ó'Direaín was forced to leave his home place and make a new life in the city, leaving behind all he knew.

Some years ago I received a phone call from a man in Co. Waterford; someone had told him I was an underwater cameraman. This man was distraught, and I couldn't understand why he'd called. He told me he was from a tiny fishing village where the fishing was gone, where he and his seven siblings had been raised on what a 27-foot trawler 'brought home'. In winter they fished herring, at other times sprat and scad, and in late summer mackerel. The situation was dire, something had to be done, someone had to do something now. And slowly it unfolded that everything this man knew, everything 'me father and me grandfather done' was gone, lost … his ability to make a living, to teach his son where the herring went in January, how to read spring tides, to battle the elements and bring home the bounty to a grateful, cheering young family, and with that, most damagingly of all, his self-esteem and identity.

My good friend Peadar Tomás Ó'Conghaile on Inis Oírr, the smallest of the Aran Islands, talks about how something radical needed to be done to save the island community and their heritage, their culture. 'Tourism is grand, but why do tourists come? They come to see our old ways, our fishing and our currachs and our culture. But the way things are, that'll be gone soon, why will tourists come then?' And if you are a young person on the Aran Islands or any other remote coastal community, the only jobs that are likely to be available will be something to do with seasonal tourism, or the diminishing small handful of fishing jobs or perhaps as a schoolteacher, educating others to follow the most likely path, which is into cities and towns. But Peadar Tomás perhaps underestimates the natural beauty and serenity of his home place, the sense of being away from the world that you get on the Arans, and the consequent draw of this to urban-dwelling office folks, ever more in need of some time to catch up with themselves.

~~~~~~

All across the world there's a tidal wave of humanity moving to the urban. This is how most of us now make a living, working in offices or factories. It's an unstoppable change in how we live, but such is the plight of the world, of subsistence, of animals and humans, food supply, hunter-gatherers, displacement, climate change and as long as there's been life there's been adaptation and evolution. 'Chaos was the law of nature, order was the dream of man,' so said American historian Samuel Adams. In my time in America I swept streets for five bucks an hour, worked as a lumberjack in Connecticut, drove a truck around Manhattan, moved furniture, worked construction – we all did, I was no different to 150,000 other Irish immigrants in 1980s America. I can recall one day moving furniture with four other Irish lads: an industrial engineer, his brother a guard on leave of absence, a plumber and a medical student, we did what we had to do to subsist. We felt fortunate to have jobs.

But we never forgot where we came from and our own people, and I can say that in all my ensuing years in computing jobs and the corporate world, I would never again have that camaraderie, craic and sense that we were all looking out for one another.

~~~~~~~~~~

My grandmother was once caught in the crossfire of an IRA ambush on British forces just outside of Kilfenora between the town of Tralee and her home place of Fenit Island. She was returning from a market on a pony and trap having sold her produce and was heavily pregnant with my father. Diving for shelter under a small cliff, I understand she actually conversed with both sides of the ambush, pleading for her life and that of my unborn father, who would later claim to have had lifelong nightmares of being shot at, though I'm not entirely convinced that may have had its origins in the ambush.

Guns were part of the vernacular in our house growing up, though mostly that of my father's. Born in 1917, he lived as a child through the war of independence and ensuing civil war and later spent three years in the Irish army during World War II, or The Emergency as it was known in Ireland.

The words 'point two two', 'double-barrel shotgun' and '303 rifle' still evoke manly memories of my father, and winter evenings

My uncle Jamie many years ago

dragging cotton wool down a shotgun barrel with builder's twine or greasing the cold metal of the weapon. Stories abounded of skirmishes and men shot in his home place of north Kerry where the ferocity of civil war left many victims and scars, some of which still remain.

Mostly though, he and his brothers shot birds and rabbits to feed themselves; a winter duck was a nutritious, fortuitous meal, and I recall delicious rabbit stews with an innate satisfaction of having hunted our own food. They even shot seabass, or tried to. A bass was a serious prize and one March, the coldest time of year in the sea, my uncle Jamie stripped off and swam out into a channel to collect a 'shot bass' – just as he approached, the creature who had likely just been stunned by the impact, came to, and swam for its life, leaving his three brothers with the lifetime ammunition of a late-night wind-up story. 'Will you be doing a bit of swimming this winter Jamie?'

My father taught me to shoot his double-barrel shotgun when I was perhaps eleven or twelve years old; I liked it and had a decent shot, I liked taking the time, breathing easily and hitting a target, though I can't recall killing anything, mostly I shot tin cans and turnips.

Sometime in the late 1970s or early '80s, my father put his shotgun away for the last time. 'Why would I shoot an animal when I can buy food in the supermarket?' he put to me one day – and then he became contrite and somewhat emotional about all the beautiful birds he'd killed, particularly the gorgeous cock pheasants, who in my opinion seem painfully, instinctually under-equipped for life in the Irish wilds.

About that time the council developed a walkway at a local lake, and it became common Sunday afternoon practice for families to drive out and park lakeside. Mallard ducks grew tame from people feeding them bread, and I can recall my father anxiously shifting from side to side in our car at the awkwardness of being within a few yards of a bounty that had for decades brought out the hunter instinct within him; he tried to laugh it off at times, but could never resist lifting his arms into a shotgun hold. 'Oh Christ, if only I had a gun.'

I had a gun pulled on me twice when I lived in New York City, scary, dangerous situations and you never know how you'll react until it happens. On the second occasion I actually started laughing, granted there was, as we say in Ireland, drink involved, but I looked the guy in the eyes and said: 'What – are you going to fucking shoot me?' I saw fear but mostly confusion come across him, and the adrenaline that had emboldened him seemed to drain away. But I was lucky.

~~~~~~~

For a year and a half in Manhattan I worked as a furniture mover and truck driver. It was tough, unstructured work, six bucks an hour, ten if you could get to be a driver plus tips, cash in hand at the end of the day. We'd call the boss in the evening and he'd gruffly bark the time we were on the next morning, six thirty Kenny, don't be late, looks like a long job, and we'd show up and stand outside a small deli on the corner of 85th Street and 1st Avenue, waiting for the truck to arrive and be called by name. One of the drivers, George, was from Hong Kong, sometimes he'd look a little bewildered calling out the names, Seamus, Sean, Mike, Tom, jeez, all you Irish guys look the same to me.

And we'd get the last few pulls on a cigarette, stand it out and climb aboard the truck for a day's hard labour. Although Manhattan is littered with skyscrapers, there are still untold ancient apartment blocks of maybe five or six storeys, many without elevators; this was what we called a 'walk-up', carrying the entire contents of someone's apartment down five floors of stairs, onto the truck and then back up at the other side, tough work in the heat and humidity of New York in July and August.

It was interesting to meet people from all walks of life, to spend a day in their home, many though were at their most stressed. One of the lads specialised in telling clients that next to bereavement, moving house was the most stressful thing we would do in our lifetime. Again and again I asked him to save it, but he couldn't seem to help himself when in the first few moments of meeting rich Americans, he had an opportunity to inform these people about their lives. We met lots of friendly folk, but most Manhattanites didn't care a toss for us, we'd kill ourselves carefully packing and moving all their furniture and worldly possessions but many would just bark at us and whinge if even the smallest thing was broken, a plate or cup or even a mark on their wall, they exhibited a sense of entitlement that I sometimes found disturbing.

I recall moving one guy from a new apartment block uptown, inhabited mostly by yuppies, a term new at the time for young, upwardly mobile individuals. The guy was a builder and obviously very successful, but in a thick Brooklyn accent he says to me, 'I tell ya buddy, people here, they think their shit don't stink,' timed nicely as a him-and-her Wall Street couple breezed past us in the corridor.

As soon as the job was done, most people wanted us out of their space, but I remember this one guy who we were told was an extremely successful surgeon, though he didn't look like one – he was tough, well-built and carried an air of humility. When we'd moved everything into his massive new penthouse on the Upper West Side, he insisted on bringing all eight of us furniture movers out onto the rooftop where he and his wife cooked up a barbecue and opened a whole case of Rolling Rock beer for us. Proudly and almost emotionally he told us how his father and all his uncles were Teamsters 'from the ground up', members of the American labour union with a long history for standing up to big business interests and fighting for workers' rights. From the 1960s to the '80s, Teamsters had stood up to the Coors beer brewery for the poor treatment of workers and alleged discrimination against minorities including Mexican–Americans and gay people. It was a long, bloody battle eventually won by the wily, obstinate beer magnate. In many bars across Connecticut and I'm sure other states, there were signs behind the bar, *No Coors sold here ever*. Some people never forget.

Towards the end of my time in New York I moved an older man out of a small dark office somewhere in midtown. He was retiring and leaving the room he'd worked in for the previous forty years as a graphic artist, held himself with great dignity and spoke in a strong, clear, but sympathetic voice. 'Computers are taking over my work I'm afraid, but it's time for me to retire anyway.' His right hand shook, not wildly, but required the steadying influence of his other hand as he wrote his signature on my bill of lading. I guess early-onset Parkinson's disease.

He asked politely if he could drive with us in the truck to his new home a couple of hours out in Long Island. We drove out of the Queens–Midtown Tunnel for the Long Island Expressway into the November night and the new chapter of this man's life and in the darkness of the cab of our truck, as squeaky windscreen wipers peeled rain back from our vision, this man told me his life story.

He'd fought in World War II, and began to tell me of boarding a troop carrier on some or other US army base in the winter of '43 or '44, they took off into the night sky, him just twenty-one, the age I was then; his comrades nicknamed him 'Pops' for being two years older than the eldest of the company.

They had no idea where they were headed, just somewhere in Europe, probably Germany or France. Many hours later the order came through to rig their parachutes and guns and within moments he was jumping out of the aircraft into the night, telling his parents out loud how he loved them and how good they'd been to him. He told me this with a slow clarity of voice, perhaps that of a man looking back and seeking to have his experience recorded in some way.

I tried to put myself in the position of jumping out of an airplane into the darkness and a waiting war zone below: this man was one of the lucky ones, he'd survived and returned home to live a normal life, but his experiences and his comrades lived strong in his consciousness. Many never came home.

I couldn't help but feel a deep sympathy for him, perhaps because his life was entering its final phase, or more likely because of the unexpressed melancholy of losing his friends in war, they who would die for him, and he for them.

'Make the most of your life son, or as much as you can,' he told me as we shook hands in farewell, and I left him to his new home on a wet November Long Island night.

COACH

'Pull on that baaalll'
He shrieks through wretched false teeth
The originals long ago
Stopped the upswing of ash
He spat them, bloodily
And stared the holder back
In that moment, the day won
And many more, to come

Through twisted fingers
Brown now, he shelters
A smouldering half Woodbine
From soft rain
Patrolling the line from 50 to 50
'Take your point Murphy'
You're better than that

Ground hurling boys,
Pull on it, the way townies do
And a half-split sliothar
Sizzled forty yards, a sweet connection
On the bás
Dirty rain water, spluttering
From its heart.

The country coaches bowed to him
They'd tested him and lost
Too many times
And watched him take Ringy for nought
In an Oireachtas Cup in March
The great one, petulant
Cleaned out by
This five-foot-five monster.

RESPONSE

I THINK MANY THINGS we do in our life are probably responses to something else, perhaps motivated by something we've encountered or felt, be that something literal or subliminal. I hear people say things like 'I just decided we were never going to be as poor as I was growing up' or 'I hated living in the city, I just had to get out of there.' Personally, this sentiment informs me how important it is to be in touch with ourselves and our heart and our loved ones, so that the things that trigger responses are truly important matters with integrity.

One of my earliest recollections of being in the sea is being washed into the caves at Ballybunion beach by a set of waves, I was maybe six or seven and went exploring, my father rescued me, he said I nearly drowned but my main recollection is of being told about what happened and being comforted by my parents and being bought chips. Later that night I decided I wanted more of those lovely salty chips and sneaked out of the funfair where I was with my family, me the youngest of eight, and with my five pence I'd been given for the bumpers, I queued up at the chip shop. As the smell wafted across the counter I could already taste them. But a large hand landed on my shoulder for the second time that day, and I was hauled back to my worried mother, my father saying, 'Oh there he was queuing up for his portion, if you don't mind.'

I resolved to be more covert.

As a young teenager I sneaked out to some of my first discos, or dances as they were in those days, with actual bands belting out rock 'n' roll. I hope my mother never discovered the rolls of clothes that were pretending to be me in my bed, but if she did, she never said anything.

~~~~~~~

When I first returned to Ireland after many years living away in cities, I couldn't get enough of the sea. All summer as soon as I finished work, I'd be in the car at 6.05 pm on my way to Lahinch or Spanish Point. One September I couldn't leave the sea. I stayed in the water for hours on a bodyboard, I didn't own a wetsuit, surfers asked me repeatedly wasn't I freezing, I couldn't leave, and I didn't. I found a way to live by the sea, and I understand perfectly the name of the classic surf movie *Endless Summer*.

Surfers and sea-lovers and most especially fishermen can't leave the sea, maybe for fear of not getting back. To paddle out to a wave and sit there in the ocean, trusting yourself to the elements, and they to you, feels like true freedom. To observe the gradations of colour in the vast expanse of an oceanic sky, and see the turquoises and blues and powdery white water as a wave breaks in front of you is a beautiful experience that screens endlessly in my dreams. The fear of being caught out when the swell kicks in with the only way back to land being to get yourself onto a meaty wave and surf it, to lose your board to a broken leash and have to swim seven or eight hundred metres through mountainous white water is as liberating as it is terrifying.

In the sea I discovered freedom, a secret garden that drew me in to explore its limitless breadth and depth, a world new to my eyes and consciousness where on every visit I would discover something new, from the smallest of creatures to how constituent parts of ecosystems worked together and how seasons brought change and breathed new life. How in winter, life would endure, always waiting and preparing for the next stage of growth or development.

It was a world for which I would take the greatest and gravest of risks, some almost unconsciously, so as to explore more and to document and articulate what I found, the magic, the murder, the viciousness, the storms and the destruction wreaked by humankind.

For the first time in my life I truly loved going to work, though I never call it that. I could never have been a marine biologist, I'd have lost interest a few pages into the textbooks and endless browbeating into students of systems and rote learning and Latin names, the distance from actual nature and lack of feeling or emotional understanding of the natural world. Even if I could have survived four years of that, I would have been a professional failure.

I found the ocean along my own journey, and though none of my ancestors who lived by and from the sea for hundreds of years ever had the privilege of seeing what I saw, of meeting the greatest, most humbling of animals, it never felt like anything other than the most natural next step to take from my early years on the seashore with my father, an island man.

When I was twelve years old, a few friends and I petrol-bombed the back of our school. There was no real damage, it was just a wall, the roof may have been singed a bit, but no one noticed, and I don't think we quite realised what we were at. One of the lads figured out how to make the bomb, a glass milk bottle, fill it up, soak a rag in petrol, light it and throw it at something … *BOOOM* … we got the fright of our young lives, I don't think we did it again or if we did, then not much. So we tried a tree … *BOOOM* … but I felt bad for the poor tree and went back often to see if it was OK – thankfully, it recovered.

Primary school was awful. For decades I would have said I didn't mind the beatings, it was the humiliation that I couldn't shake off, but in retrospect I was wrong, the beatings were bad. They defended it as the school culture of the time. How a grown man can beat up a nine- or ten-year-old child and not comprehend that this is wrong is unfathomable. But all across Ireland it happened, they got away with murder, in some cases literally. Keeping discipline and order in a class of forty kids is no easy feat, but that is the job of a teacher, and every job has its challenges. I had more good teachers than bad, and not every school had that level of violence or lack of respect for children.

Coming from a family full of teachers I'm familiar with the challenges of teaching; my older sister Margaret's first job was teaching fifty-three junior infants in Finglas, how she managed I don't know but she did.

For previous generations it was even worse, school should have been an education, and for kids with tough homes, a refuge or sanctuary even. Instead it was the polar opposite. I've met too many men scarred and trying to shake off the terror and humiliation of what they suffered as children, most all of it thoughtless humiliation of children in front of their peers, often due to a teacher's inability to gain respect or retain self-control.

When parents of kids with privileged backgrounds arrived to our headmaster, he would literally dance around them, yet I can still see him sneering at mothers from difficult circumstances before they'd even opened their mouths, they just didn't have the self-confidence to defend themselves. My own mother was confident enough to stand up to him, she had suffered her own terrible experiences at school and later also with my older siblings. But we never told our parents what was happening to us at school, and perhaps like a lot of victims, we had been convinced that what happened was our fault, that we were the ones in the wrong and we carried this as shame and guilt into our adult lives.

Once I was caught drawing 'dirty pictures' on a schoolbook, actually the brown paper cover I myself had made to protect the book. I wasn't in fact caught – the guy next to me was caught doing something and in return for immunity, he grassed me up. I was never much good at drawing; it was a rough outline of a body with a woman's boobs. That it was a religion book seemingly made my sin particularly grave, for the teacher felt the judgement was above his court and quietly sent me to the headmaster.

It got worse and worse. I was first slapped around the head in a private session in his office. He would push his gold ring over his finger knuckle, as if a finger knuckle wasn't hard enough, and get you on the side of the head, sometimes the temple. I was then dragged by my ear back to the class of forty-four other kids, and for more than half an hour the class was given a sanctimonious lecture by Mr Head about how our bodies are the temple of the Holy Ghost, and because of this the devil would try to tempt us with sex, Mr Head pointing at me for these parts of his sermon as I stood alone and crying at the front of the class. On he went, alternating between good, while facing the class, and bad, while facing me. I was ten years old.

Walking home at lunchtime I must have looked a bit shell-shocked, because one of the lads said to the fella with me, 'What's up with yer man?' 'Oh he just got a forty-minute lecture about sex and his body from the headmaster.' 'Feck it,' says the other guy, 'why didn't we get that?'

It spilled over to the school yard. I was a half a foot taller than my peers. 'Ó'Súilleabháin, you long lanky weed' one of my teachers would taunt me, the same man giving us lectures about not putting cruel nicknames onto lads. I was picked on and beaten up by older boys; I wasn't as strong as them or perhaps didn't have the confidence to stand up to them. And I became a bully too.

At times, I drank a lot during my twenties, usually when vis-it-ing home at Christmas and trying to catch up with friends. Maybe I just liked partying, but I sometimes wondered what was wrong with me, though all the lads I grew up with did the same. Some still do. But I also worked ridiculously hard. In New York, twelve-hour days were the norm. Once we worked forty hours al-most straight, which included twenty hours of driving a truck – it's amazing to think there were no controls on truck drivers' driving time back then. I managed a single hour's sleep after unloading the truck and before facing into the ten-hour drive from upstate New York back to the city. Coming down the Major Deegan Expressway, about an hour from the city and thirty-nine hours into my own journey, a woman suddenly changed lanes in front of us but I somehow managed to hit the brakes in time to avoid her. Why didn't I understand that I should never have been in that place?

In London I worked in computing on trading floors for seven years, pin-striped suits, money and egos. I felt it was a great job, and maybe it was, it certainly took years of twelve-hour days and learning my skills to get to that level, but the traders and banks made all the money; we were near the bottom of the food chain. I used to say I loved it at the time, though I'm not convinced now – it was suffocating and lacking in humanity, but the thought of doing something for a living that you could love never seemed realistic, it was always just about getting and keeping a job. In my last year there, work was literally never-ending, and from January to June we had just two weekends off, working all the others, with an occasional day off midweek as compensation. We thought this was the norm. One day I couldn't work anymore, my body just said no, I got as far as my desk, looked at the guy beside me and blurted out, 'I'm fucked, I have to go home.' I was emotionally drained from exhaustion, so they gave me a week off. I told them I was going to Margate to recover, instead, I took a flight to Paris and hid out there for a week with a beautiful girl I knew. Maybe

I'd finally gotten sense. I came back recovered and began my journey back home to Ireland.

~~~~~~~

I'd played in bands since I was sixteen, there's no better feeling than playing music with your mates, the count-in, 2–3–4, boom, the music. I loved writing music and trying to get better as a band. One of our highlights was a gig we played in our school hall a month before the Leaving Cert. It was a beautiful early summer's evening, the hall was unexpectedly – and inexplicably to us – jammed with three hundred teenagers, we weren't Pink Floyd, but we weren't bad either. When we played Floyd's 'Another Brick in the Wall', the place went bananas, I mean, there was this communal release of teenage angst.

I was heartbroken not to have been able to make a living from music. After two years in New York trying to make it, reality dawned, and I moved to London to get a 'real' job. But I missed music so much, I think I turned my back on it at that point, perhaps in selfish anger, and didn't play a whole lot for years, but when it's in you, you have to express it.

The council built a huge estate of houses next to us when I was a child, it opened a new road into a bunch of other estates and in just a few months we went from living surrounded by green fields and ancient trees to living in the midst of hundreds of houses and people. One summer we were playing in this huge underground pipe system they were constructing, it must have been a storm drain or sewer but was big enough to stand up in. Coming out into the blinding light we heard a strange, bizarre sound, one of the lads called out 'The rock boys! The rock boys!' and almost unsure why, we were running towards the sound, down a laneway with semi-derelict houses on one side and where the ancient buildings of Carmody Street backed onto the other: from within one of these crumbling buildings a snare drum sizzled up across warm summer air, the bass and an electric guitar rose up and caught the rhythm and a muffled voice joined the party doing its best to be Rory Gallagher or Dr Feelgood. This was 1970s Ireland and I was caught, it was creativity, erotic and sexy, and seeped through my consciousness promising all kinds of liberation, and perhaps even escape.

I stood in a field on a hill somewhere between Doolin and Lisdoonvarna one hot summer evening in the 1980s, barely a teenager. Three men walked on stage, a band I didn't know much of, kind of folky trad, but they looked cool. Sonny Condell began to gyrate his upper body and the monstrous stage-side speakers belted out a hornpipe rhythm – from an acoustic guitar? What was this …

'Wake up farm boys! The barn is burning down!' du duddle du dum, du duddle du dum, the hornpipe rhythm reaching forward like some folk militia marching band rising up the people in a rebel response to some long-suffered oppression. And we stood eyes and mouths wide open, what was this? The band played on, a magic now seeping across all the watching souls.

Then all went quiet. One of the three, a moustachioed man with a flock of brown curls, approached the microphone and began blowing into something we were later to discover was a blues harmonica. There was a terrible shriek that waivered, lingered and screamed across the fields as our minds struggled to comprehend its exotic wailing sound … a banshee, it rose up to challenge the gods of traditional music across this sacred musical landscape that is North Clare, where the Russells and Killougherys replayed and released the music of peoples past, of the piper alone at the cliffs, and suffering and loss, mirth and dance and human love and happiness. And all at once the fairy gods of music seemed to rise together, and maybe bow and dance across the Atlantic sky. Hairs rose on our necks and the lone voice wailed, '*going up t'country where the water it tastes like wine …*'

Foreign music it might be, raising imagery of trains and travel and hobos, men running away, of women, love and pain, but this, this was legitimate magic, and in that moment the 60,000 other people standing spellbound beside me rose up on a journey of the mind, as so many of our ancestors had done along the shores of Moher and Doolin for hundreds of years, responding to the Atlantic storms and ceaseless wind and rain and hardness of life with music and magic and love.

They credited the fairies, and maybe they were right, but I think it came from the ether of their own consciousness and the spirit memory of their ancestors and released them from the forlorn. It was manna from heaven and delicate hope, addictive and dangerous.